PUT OPTION PROFITS

HOW TO TURN TEN MINUTES OF FREE TIME INTO CONSISTENT CASH FLOW EACH MONTH

TRAVIS WILKERSON

WWW.TRADERTRAVIS.COM

TABLE OF CONTENTS

Preface   9
Introduction   13

1. TRIGGER WARNING   21
   Outrageous Investment Returns

2. STOCK OPTIONS SIMPLIFIED   31
   What Are Stock Options?   34

3. BUFFETT'S SECRET STRATEGY   45
   Selling Put Options
   Getting Paid to Buy Stocks: A Million-Dollar
   Put Selling Example   48

4. INTRO TO PUT CREDIT SPREADS   55
   Making Buffett's Insurance Trade Less Risky   56
   The Two Types of Credit Spread Trades   62

5. BUFFETT'S BILLION-DOLLAR INCOME
   TRADE   67
   Stock Options Versus Index Options   68

6. HOW TO OPEN AND CLOSE A PUT
   CREDIT SPREAD   81
   What Type of Account Will You Need?   82
   Selling a Put Credit Spread   83
   Buying Back a Put Credit Spread   89

7. THE POPULAR BUT DANGEROUS WAY OF
   SELLING CREDIT SPREADS   95
   Another Reason I Don't Sell High-
   Probability Spreads   104

8. THE UNCONVENTIONAL BUT MORE
   PROFITABLE WAY OF SELLING SPREADS   109
   OTM Versus ATM Credit Spreads   110
   Dollar Cost Average Credit Spreads   112
   The Secret to Long-Term ATM Spreads   113

9. A PROVEN CASH FLOW TEMPLATE   119
   My Four-Step Passive Income Blueprint   122

10. SHOWING YOU THE MONEY   133
    Your Proof-of-Concept Exercise   135

11. QUESTIONS ABOUT MANAGING CREDIT
    SPREADS   145
    The Complicated Way of Determining Profit 146
    The Simple Way of Determining Profit   148
    Additional Management Questions   150

12. MISCELLANEOUS CREDIT SPREAD
    QUESTIONS   159

    BONUS   175
    Enhanced Buy-and-Hold Income
    Profit Is Income, and Income Is Profit   177
    Bonus: The Naked Put Tweak (For
    Experienced Put-Sellers Only)   181
    EBHI Performance Estimates   186

    Final Thoughts   191
    References   197
    About the Author   199

HOW TO GET THE MOST OUT OF THIS BOOK

Books are great, but sometimes, you need additional resources to deepen your learning experience. Thus, I have put together a bonus package for readers of this book, where you will gain access to the following FREE resources:

- A seven-module option basics **video course**.
- A live case study of the **cash flow blueprint** taught in this book. You will see how I, a US investing champion, make real-time decisions.
- You'll also gain access to my **trade journal in Excel**. This way, you can view the history of my trades and my current positions.

You will also get my emails with your case study. I share my favorite option trading strategies, ways to protect your investments in any market, and complimentary alerts about trades I will place. All these bonuses are 100  percent free, with no strings attached. You only need to enter your email address.

To get your bonuses, go to www.tradertravis.com/book bonus.html. Alternatively, you can scan the QR code.

PREFACE

> *When obstacles arise, you change your direction to reach your goal. You do not change your decision to get there.*
>
> — ZIG ZIGLAR

This is the third and final book in the *Passive Stock Options Trading* series. The first book, *Options Trading Made Simple*, covered stock options basics and dispelled a few myths about options—specifically, the misconception that options are risky and should be avoided by average investors. It then showed a proven path to achieving financial freedom in five years with options. Finally, for proof of concept, the book profiled an active trading strategy where you enter and exit trades at various times. This is also known as timing the stock market, or market timing for short.

However, in that book, I stated that although active trading is more popular, you should strongly consider passive investing because it's much simpler. That's precisely why I've retired from active trading and am now a passive options investor. Another reason I stopped active trading is that life got in the way! More specifically, here are some challenges I've faced and how they've shaped my perspective.

- I had (and still have) kid challenges.
- My wife almost filed for a divorce.
- I had a personal health scare.
- One brother had a stroke.
- Another had cancer.
- And my dad died.

In addition to the above, I had to care for my disabled mom, who had early signs of dementia. And oh, she also died shortly after. For a while, my life was a dumpster fire, and those life events caused me to struggle with active stock market trading. My performance started to suffer, which affected my ability to earn income and provide for my family.

Active trading requires focus, lots of free time, and mental clarity, all of which I did not have while dealing with the chaos of life. Eventually, I started making less money with active trading than my wife's simple buy-and-hold approach to investing. However, one good thing came from my misfortunes: During the above turmoil, I prayed for a way to make money that gave me more free time to focus on being a better husband and father. I was then blessed with insights that helped me develop a new, passive way of investing that allows one to rapidly build wealth while living free from the worry of market crashes.

The second book, *10-Minute Options Trading and ETF Investing*, covered that new and improved approach: enhanced buy-and-hold, or EBH for short. Best of all, implementing it only takes a few minutes a year. Even though I was initially skeptical about beating the stock market average with a strategy that only takes ten minutes, I discovered it is possible. That book even demonstrated this with a case study where readers watched a couple grow their $10,000 account into nearly half a million dollars.

Despite EBH's success, one negative bothered me for years. With active trading and a $100,000 account, I generated a monthly income of $2,000 to $4,000. However, passive investing didn't produce the consistent monthly income I used to earn with active trading. I needed more income but no longer had the energy or desire to trade actively. I had to find a way to earn a consistent monthly income while still adhering to the passive ten-minute investing style. After much testing and tweaking, I finally came up with a solution, and I'm sharing that method in this book.

You'll discover an investment strategy that produces consistent cash flow and takes only ten minutes a month to implement. You can withdraw the money from your account to spend or leave it in there to compound. This book is the final piece of the trifecta. By diligently studying and implementing the principles outlined in this series, you will gain the skills and strategies necessary for massive account growth, consistent monthly income, and market crash protection.

Here's to your future success,
Travis Wilkerson
The 10-Minute Investor™ & 2019 US Investing Champion (Options Division)

INTRODUCTION

> *The way to get started is to quit talking and begin doing.*
>
> — WALT DISNEY

This book is about making money in the stock market in less time and with less effort than conventional employment. More specifically, it's written for the millions of people trapped in the cycle of going to work, getting money, paying bills, having no money, and repeating the process. It's an exhausting routine of trading your time for money throughout your entire working life. Then, if you have kids, they get into the same system, and the cycle of bondage is repeated. It's surviving, not thriving.

Trading time for dollars is a good way to earn a living, but it is also a difficult way to build wealth because there is only so much time you can work. If that's your current way of earning money, how's that working out for you? Are you financially free? Do you have investments that produce enough cash flow to cover your life expenses? If you do, congratulations—you're part of the 1 percent. However, this book is not for you. It's for the 99 percent of the population still trapped in the cycle of trading time for money. Or worse, those forced into a retirement they're not financially prepared for.

This book is deeply personal to me. I'm a one percenter who, despite growing up poor, was fortunate enough to have been able to opt out of the corporate rat race at a young age. However, I am surrounded by family and friends who are still trapped, and I'm painfully aware that not everyone is as lucky. This realization fuels my mission to share my escape plan with as many people as possible so they can break the shackles of financial bondage. It's what someone did for me over three decades ago.

And that leads to the big promise of this book: Within these pages, you will discover how to generate passive income from selling stock insurance. It's how **you can turn ten minutes of free time into consistent cash flow each month.** The methods are perfect for those who fear they won't have enough money in retirement or those who want a second income without getting a second job. And yes, I know this will sound unbelievable, especially to working-class individuals. No one has shown them another way to provide for their family. Working hard for money is all they know. I don't fault them for thinking it's the only way to make money. Heck, I used to think that way until I was lucky enough to meet a rich person who showed me simple ways of creating multiple streams of income from the stock market.

But let me be clear: Simple does not mean easy! There is nothing easy about achieving financial freedom. It's a long and grueling financial marathon, but it is doable for most people. But how exactly do you build wealth while earning a consistent monthly income—even if you have little free time and desperately want to give up your nine-to-five job? It's simple. You will work smart, not hard.

You could spend years trying to figure things out on your own, or you could copy someone already successful. You are more likely to succeed if you copy those who are already successful at what you want to do. That is precisely why the students with "D" grades try to copy off those with "A" grades in school. In grade school, copying others is seen as wrong. However, in adult life, it's often the more intelligent approach. That's why you will model the strategy of someone already wealthy.

The person we are modeling is highly respected in the investment industry. He's a billionaire who currently serves as the co-founder, chairman, and CEO of Berkshire Hathaway. You may have heard of him before: His name is

Warren Buffett (Wikipedia contributors 2024). Everyone knows Buffett as a stock investor, but did you know he also uses a secret options strategy? I say it's a secret because people rarely talk about it.

In the following chapters, you'll learn all about options trading and Buffett's approach, but you don't have to be a billionaire to benefit from this strategy. Ordinary investors can use it, too. However, most won't. They avoid options because they listen to financial experts who vilify stock option contracts (i.e., derivatives). Most investors are told to avoid derivatives because they are risky and complicated. Sometimes, they even tell you a story about someone who lost all their money trading options.

Also, some people wrongly assume that Warren Buffett hates options because, in the 2002 Berkshire Hathaway shareholder letter, he wrote: "In our view, however, derivatives are financial weapons of mass destruction, carrying dangers that, while now latent, are potentially lethal." The irony in that statement is that in the same letter, he also says, "Indeed, at Berkshire, I sometimes engage in large-scale derivatives transactions in order to facilitate certain investment strategies." In the 2008 shareholder letter, you discover what he meant by "large-scale." Here's a quote from that letter:

66 *Our first contract comes due on September 9, 2019, and our last on January 24, 2028. We have received premiums of $4.9 billion, money we have invested. We, meanwhile, have paid nothing, since all expiration dates are far in the future. (Shareholder Letters n.d.)*

As you can see, Berkshire Hathaway has made billions of dollars in profit using these "weapons of mass destruction." And the strategy you'll learn in this book is a slight variation of Buffett's billion-dollar option trade. So, if you ever hear people say stock options are risky and you should stay away from them, I want you to remember that one of the world's most respected and highly conservative investors uses options. That said, I do, however, agree that options trading, like all investing, has a risk of massive loss. However, just because someone else was an idiot and gambled with options doesn't mean you have to be dumb like them.

I suggest you follow Berkshire Hathaway's prudent approach to options. They sell stock insurance contracts, commonly referred to as put options. I've been investing for nearly three decades, and I'm still surprised at how many people don't use these contracts, even though they've existed since the late 1970s. Investors buy this type of insurance to protect themselves from losing large sums of money in the stock market. This book will reveal how to make money from selling this type of insurance to them.

You will enter the insurance business like Buffett, but you won't be selling car or home insurance. You will sell stock insurance, something many worldwide do not know exists. It's a shame because they are missing out on the passive income you can earn from selling it and the peace of mind you can have from buying this insurance to protect your investment portfolio. Selling stock insurance is a reliable and lower-risk way to profit with options, and it doesn't take hundreds of thousands of dollars to start this business. In a later chapter, I'll show you how you can begin this passive income business with as little as $5,000.

If that sounds like an outrageous claim, I understand. However, if you can suspend your skepticism for the short time it takes to read this book, I think you will see an entirely new world opening up for you and your family that you didn't even know existed. Before that can happen, though, I have to clear up a few misconceptions about options because, as I have already shared, some people believe that options are dangerous and should not be used by average investors. The truth is that options were created to lower the risk of investing.

That fact aside, others feel that options are complicated and hard to understand. If that's you, I have good news. You don't need to be good at math, have a degree in engineering, or be a genius to understand options. Anyone with basic common sense can learn how to make money with options. At least the way taught in this book.

In summary, learning how to make money with options is a skill. Like any skill, it takes time to learn. If you want to develop the ability to earn five, six, or even seven figures a year in passive income, you must push through the challenges of learning options. However, that dream lifestyle will never happen if you get overwhelmed and quit. So, take your time and review the concepts as often as needed. If you do that, it will slowly start to make more sense.

What helps even more is practicing the concepts. Think about swimming: Is reading a book about it the best way to learn it, or is it getting in the water and practicing it for real? It's the same with investing. Reading is great, but applying what you learn is even better. **Taking action is the only way to achieve the book's promises.**

Please commit to putting in at least six months of effort to learn this skill. If you do that, I'm confident a financial miracle will occur in your life. So, make that promise to yourself right now. I want you to silently commit to yourself that you will read this book and apply these concepts for at least six months. If you aren't happy with the results, you can return to life as usual.

However, I predict that once you get a taste of the profit potential of options, you will be hooked for life. There is something magical and addictive about clicking a few buttons and watching instant cash hit your account. If you have ten minutes, a way to connect to the internet, and the ability to click a few buttons, you can transform that into a consistent stream of passive income. It sounds like hype, but it's a fact. That said, let's dive deeper into this journey so you can learn how to generate consistent cash flow with this weird-sounding tool called stock options.

1

TRIGGER WARNING

OUTRAGEOUS INVESTMENT RETURNS

> *Some people want it to happen, some people wish it would happen, others make it happen.*

— MICHAEL JORDAN

As you learned in the introduction, the book's primary purpose is to show how we can model Warren Buffett's approach to selling stock insurance (i.e., put options). More specifically, you will discover how to sell **put credit spreads**. The geeky name of the strategy will be explained later in the book, but it's an income-generating strategy that can produce hundreds to thousands in monthly income. This money can be used to travel the world, upgrade your lifestyle, or support charitable causes. On the more practical side, perhaps you need to fund retirement, pay for a kid's college, or reduce your financial anxiety.

If you need more income, credit spreads can help. Here's a rough estimate of how much a person can earn once they master the skill of options investing. These are potential earnings estimates based on what I occasionally achieve (your results will vary):

- $10,000 account size: potential monthly earnings of $100 to $200
- $50,000 account size: potential monthly earnings of $500 to $1,000
- $100,000 account size: potential monthly earnings of $1,000 to $2,000
- $250,000 account size: potential monthly earnings of $2,500 to $5,000
- $500,000 account size: potential monthly earnings of $5,000 to $10,000

To be clear, I do not guarantee you will achieve profits like this. I will, however, show you exactly how I do it. Also, if those returns seem too good to be true, I get it. That's why I'm not asking for your trust and faith immediately. I only ask that you temporarily suspend any disbelief long enough to try these concepts out for yourself.

Nevertheless, I hope those income examples inspire those who think they need millions to retire comfortably. I also hope you're not affected by the mind virus called skepticism because if you are, you'll never achieve returns like the ones just shared. I shared my performance online, and it made several people angry. Below is a small sample of the responses I received. **Warning:** If you think this way, <u>you will fail</u> with the strategy taught in this book:

> *There is ZERO chance of this being true...Nobody gets consistent returns like that. Warren Buffett doesn't. That is better than what Bernie Madoff promised with his Ponzi Scheme ... Nobody can get 24+ percent returns a year consistently.*

> *No way. This is not possible at all. You will go broke fast following whatever strategy is suggested here. I assume the option that is being sold to achieve these results is using crappy meme stocks with very high volatility.*

> *... Impossible to make this consistently month after month long-term.*

> *Don't believe this guy. You are not going to make 36 percent a year trading options.*

> *So, you are saying you are better than Stanley Druckenmiller in generating returns? Got it.*

Everyone is entitled to their opinion, but the investors who wrote those comments won't succeed with what this book teaches. They are ignorant in the traditional sense. They don't know what they don't know, and they will never experience the profit potential of credit spreads because they are too close-minded and skeptical. I'm speaking from experience because I used to be just as mistrustful; however, I got counseling to help me over-come my limiting beliefs. Once my skeptical mind virus was eradicated, I started accomplishing things people said were impossible.

For instance, I meet many people who think it's impossible to consistently beat the stock market's performance. In every one of these situations, their investment results match that belief. Compare that to Warren Buffett. Warren didn't become a billionaire by thinking like the people above. He believed that higher returns were possible, and he manifested that reality. I have noticed that a person's reality almost always matches what they think is possible. I know that sounds all *woo-woo*, but it's what I have observed in my nearly three decades of investing.

Here's another non-investing-related example to demon-strate this point. Have you ever seen a person win a gold medal in the Olympics and then say they were surprised they won because they didn't think it was possible? **Out of belief comes reality.** For example, some people don't believe you can turn ten minutes of free time into consis-tent cash flow. Thus, they will never experience the joy of doing it. I feel bad for them because it is possible, and I only discovered that because I dared to believe it could be done.

I also firmly believe I can outperform the market in most years, so my reality usually matches my belief. However, maybe I've been lucky all these years and will eventually lose my money. Or, maybe winning the US Investing Championship was a fluke. Only time will tell. All I know is that I keep achieving what people tell me is dumb luck or impossible.

However, I don't know you or your work ethic. I offer no guarantees or promises of what you can achieve. I'm just here documenting my strategies and hope to inspire other big dreamers who are willing to believe that the above returns are achievable. I'm not even asking you to believe it naively. I'm asking you to be intellectually curious and do what the US Army taught me: "Trust, but verify." You trust that it's true, but verify it to be sure.

If you verify the simple blueprint revealed in a later chapter, you will see that it is possible to generate consistent income, but it won't be every single month. Stock market returns don't work that way. Those income examples have a wide range because the stock market can be temperamental. Your income and performance will vary based on how the market is performing. Sometimes, you will make money, and sometimes, you will lose, but the goal is to make money overall.

Also, if you "trust but verify," here is another odd bit you will discover: Learning the technical aspects of making money will be the easy part of your journey. Even though the steps outlined in this book will sound simple, achieving financial freedom will be challenging. For some odd reason, life gets harder when you try to better yourself. It's almost as if the universe tests you to see how badly you want success.

Said another way, life will get in the way; it happens to all of us. When—not if, but when it happens—remember that you are an investor, and just like a stock price, there will be highs and lows in your life. Everyone falls at some point in their life. The losers stay down and whine about their misfortune. The winners fall and get back up. That cycle of failing but trying again is how you win the game of investing.

Motivational lesson aside, I want you to understand that I'm spending so much time on mindset because I've repeatedly seen how a person's mindset and belief system are the real reason they are held back financially. For example, I'm a former US investing champion with several decades of successful investing experience. Yet, people constantly attack me and say my methods won't work. Sadly, they never realize their skepticism (due to their mindset) hurts them, not me. Their disbelief doesn't change my truth; those performance examples shown are based on actual credit spread trades my family makes.

I taught my wife and young kids how to start one of these stock insurance businesses. It's important to note that they are not as passionate about trading options as I am.

They also don't have an expert understanding, but they can follow the simple four-step instructions I gave them. By selling put credit spreads, **they consistently make $1,400 a month.** And yes, there is the potential to make much more money. That's just what they earn as beginners with a relatively small account. So, I hope their success encourages you to learn this valuable money-making skill, which can help you generate an extra income stream. You'll learn the strategy's "how-to" in a later chapter, but let me show you one of the put trades my wife and kids recently placed.

$SPX Vertical Put Spre...	FILLED	Buy	1/1	Credit $14.15	Day	$14.20	$12.00	$13.65	$15.30	3:18 PM 08/19/2024
SPX 03/21/2025 5550.00 P	FILLED	Buy to Open	1 -	-		$174.62	$171.70	$172.50	$173.30	3:18 PM 08/19/2024
SPX 03/21/2025 5600.00 P	FILLED	Sell to Open	1 -	-		$188.82	$185.30	$186.15	$187.00	3:18 PM 08/19/2024

Figure 1: Example of a put credit spread my wife recently placed, Source: Schwab.com

I know this transaction will look weird and complicated to newer investors. However, you will quickly get used to how they look and will enjoy seeing them hit your investment account each month. The transaction in Figure 1 is what I fondly call my wife's put option paycheck. The stock market paid her $1,415 in potential income for doing ten minutes of work, and this is what you will learn how to do in this book. In the options world, the "paycheck" just shown is known as a long-term at-the-money put credit spread. If you already have some experience with credit spreads, the above is an unconventional method I haven't seen taught elsewhere.

You'll discover why we take this approach in the later chapters. However, let me talk to the novice investors for a moment. If you're new to options, the term "at-the-money put credit spread" may sound confusing, and all those numbers may look intimidating. Your head trash may be surfacing, and a little voice might whisper: *This is already too complicated. I don't think I'll be able to learn this.* If that's close to what you were thinking, I have a question: How can you honestly know if this will be too complicated unless you first try it?

I'm confident that if you stick with me and slowly read the entire book, you will understand the above option gibberish by the end. You'll go from not knowing a thing about credit spreads to being able to place trades yourself. Again, the "how to" of placing these trades will be shared later in the book, but the following is an overview of the work you will perform each month. Do you think you can handle this simple process?

1. If stock market conditions are favorable, you will go into your account each month and sell a put credit spread. It takes about ten minutes, and you're done until next month.
2. Since you're selling insurance to someone, cash will be instantly deposited into your account.
3. If the stock market behaves (which it usually does), you'll get to keep all the money. If not, you'll incur a small but manageable loss.

The unique feature of this type of insurance trade is that you can decide when you want to get paid. Some people chose to get paid every week, some every month, and others every year. The income earned is like a paycheck from a job—a means to an end. Except for this job, there is no employment application to fill out, no job fair line to stand in, and no humiliating interview where you feel like you are begging and performing so someone can hire you. Also, no unfair performance evaluations or incompetent managers will hinder your success. It's just you against the stock market.

It's a relatively simple job, with no limit to how much you can make, and it only takes a few minutes a month to perform. You don't have to become a world-famous guru or fall in love with options like I did. Trust me, my wife did not. She said options investing is too boring—the only reason she trades options is because her overly persistent husband harassed her for fourteen years to learn it. But hey, I'm not complaining. Credit spread profits give her extra money, and her frugal husband is less uptight about her spending habits.

Before we move on, one last bit of wisdom: By studying how to succeed with options, you add another task to your already busy life. Your life will get harder before it improves, but there is no shortcut to doing the grueling work. No magic wealth fairy will deposit money into your account. If you want to generate consistent income from the stock market, you'll need to put in the time to learn and practice the skill. This is what you'll need to commit:

- A few hours to learn the strategy (the more, the better)
- Ten to twenty minutes once a month to implement it
- Then, at least six months of consistent action will be needed to create a second income stream

That's it! It's extremely doable, in my biased opinion. However, if you aren't willing to commit to bettering your life, no book can help you. But if you are ready and willing to make a positive change in your life, let's move on to the next chapter. We'll discuss the basics of stock options, and you'll see that they are not complicated or hard to understand.

2

STOCK OPTIONS SIMPLIFIED

> *Because of stock options, I go to bed every night without worrying about what the stock market will do.*
>
> — PETER M.

The approaches to options covered in my first two books were using options to make money—whether the stock market goes up or down—and using options as market crash insurance to protect your accounts if the stock market falls in price. Finally, there is an approach that profits from stocks trading sideways or going nowhere in price: Selling put credit spreads. It's one of the best ways to generate passive stock market income.

Unlike passive income from real estate, there are no tenants to deal with, toilets to fix, or roofs to replace. It's just you printing money from anywhere in the world with just a few taps on your phone. Sounds incredible, right? Although that is a reality for some, what's conveniently rarely discussed is all the obstacles you must overcome before making all this life-changing money. There is a hurdle between where you are now and where you want to be (generating passive income each month). That hurdle is education—being educated about options and how to use them properly.

We will start with the basics of stock options. Then, in the later chapters, you'll discover the tactics, strategies, and step-by-step blueprints that will show you how to make money with options. However, before I explain what options are, I want to take a moment to discuss the most frustrating aspect of options education. The industry has weird and intimidating vocabulary to learn before the concepts make sense. It's why options are confusing and make zero sense to most people. When those curious about options hear terms like "black-Scholes," "gamma," and "theta," they shake their heads and say, "Nope, options are not for me. It sounds too complicated." They get over-whelmed, quit, and never experience the incredible benefits of options.

That's why I'll try to use simple terms you will under-stand. Still, if you get overwhelmed by options terminol-ogy, I want you to remember that every specialized industry has its own language. The options trading community is no different, so don't get intimidated by the jargon of options. Instead, think about it this way: The medical field, the airline industry, and even teenagers all have unique jargon they use.

My teenage sons say words like "drippy" (dressing stylishly) and "glazing" (winning someone's approval by over-praising or kissing butt). Their most frequent term used is "bruh." It's a multi-use word with different meanings, but they usually say it when I do something to annoy them. For example: "Dad, can I play basketball with my friends?" I respond, "Sure if you wash the dishes and clean your room first." Their reply: "Bruh!"

Here is the point: If you want to communicate with teenagers, you should learn their language. Likewise, to build significant wealth and increase your family's financial security, you need to understand the language of money—even if the terminology initially seems weird and confusing. Your other option is to stay ignorant and struggle with money all your life. The choice is yours.

In addition to the educational hurdle, you also have to overcome a mental hurdle. Your negative head trash may convince you that options are complicated and hard to comprehend. The truth is that you don't need to be a genius to succeed with options. You can understand stock options if you are familiar with buying cars or car insurance. People often don't believe me when I say that, so I'll prove it in this chapter as we cover stock options basics.

Before we begin, though, here's a quick note: If you've read any of my previous books or are familiar with stock options basics, feel free to skim through this chapter. However, the later chapters are written assuming you have thoroughly reviewed this information. Also, unlike some option fanatics, I won't geek out on terminology and every aspect of options. I'll touch on the big-picture overview, so you understand the purpose of why options were created.

Think of it like teaching you how to drive a car without teaching you how the car's engine works. After all, what's more useful to you, learning how to drive (i.e., making money) or learning how an engine works (i.e., geeky knowledge that's not needed)? Stated another way, do you want to feel smart or make money? If you said you want to make money, the following explanations are for you.

WHAT ARE STOCK OPTIONS?

A stock option, or option for short, is a contract or agreement between two people where one person agrees to deliver something (e.g., stock shares) to another person within a specific time and for a particular price. If you're the option contract buyer, you have the right to buy or sell 100 shares of stock. Those contract rights may not seem profound, but they help you manage the risk of losing money in the stock market. So, in summary, options are risk management tools. This is quite ironic because many people believe that options are risky. As you'll see in a moment, options aren't dangerous; ignorance is.

The Two Types of Options Contracts

There are only two types of option contracts: purchase and sales contracts. The book's core focus will be sales contracts, but let me quickly cover purchase contracts for reference only. Pretend there is a stock you want to buy; it's priced at $300. If you purchase 100 shares, it will cost $30,000. However, you are scared to buy it because the stock market is at all-time highs, and you're worried that the stock may fall in price as soon as you buy it. You are emotionally conflicted because it could also rise in price to $600, and you don't want to miss out on the potential profit.

Luckily, a solution was created to help you with this predicament. **It's a tool that reduces the risk of buying stocks outright.** Instead of buying the stock, you can buy a purchase contract for $1,000. This unique option contract grants you the right to buy the stock for $300. One downfall is that you have a limited time to do this. The contract and the rights that come with it eventually expire.

Regardless, if the stock does, in fact, rise in price to $600, you can exercise the rights of the contract and buy it for the cheaper cost of $300. It would be like having a stock coupon for 50 percent off. Per the contract terms, the person who sold you the call option would be obligated to sell you those stock shares at the agreed-upon $300 price. However, if the stock never rises and instead falls to $150 (a 50 percent decline), you never use the option contract. You'd walk away happy that you only lost the $1,000 paid for the option versus the $15,000 you would have lost if you bought the stock outright.

The tool that allows you to do this is called a **call option** (or "call" for short). Don't stress about the weird name. Just roll with it. Once I break options down more, you will learn to ignore the odd names and focus on what the tool does: Call options are purchase contracts. They let you make a small downpayment, so you can only buy stocks once they have proven themselves to be money-makers.

Another type of purchase contract you may be familiar with is a car contract, which lets you purchase a vehicle for a set price. For instance, if the contract is for a $30,000 vehicle, the buyer can buy the car at that price, and the seller is obligated to sell at that price. Can you see how this is similar to a call option? The buyer can purchase something at a set price, and the seller must sell it at that price.

The second type of stock option is a sales contract that acts like an insurance policy for your investment account. It's a contract in which, in exchange for a fee, another person agrees to compensate you in the event of a loss. Using the previous example, let's say you didn't buy a call option but instead outright purchased 100 shares of stock XYZ for $300. You also buy an insurance contract, which allows you to sell the stock for $300, even if the stock crashes in price to $150. **In other words, this contract protects you from losing money during market crashes.**

A **put option** (or "put" for short) is the tool that allows you to do this. Buying a put option "guarantees" you can sell 100 shares of your stock at whatever price you choose. This sales price is called the "exercise or **strike price**" of the put. In our example, the sales or strike price is $300. So, if you buy a stock for $300 and want protection against a market crash, you can buy a put option that guarantees you can sell the stock for $300.

Before we move on, here is a quick lesson on making money with put options. When stocks fall in price, put options become more valuable in the marketplace, which increases their cost. So the person who bought the put will make money, and the person who sold the put would lose money. It works in reverse also. Insurance is less valuable if stock prices rise because it's unnecessary. So if the stock increases in price, the person who bought the put will lose money, and the person who sold the put will make money.

Now let's return to our example: Pretend stock XYZ crashed in price. As a put buyer, you have two choices: sell the put for a profit, offsetting what you are losing on your stock shares, or exercise it. If you decide to exercise the rights of your contract (the right to sell), the put seller must buy your stock from you at the agreed-upon strike price.

Now you understand why options exist, and I hope you can see how ignorance of their benefits is the real risk. After all, investing in the stock market is one of the best ways to get rich. However, many people fear investing because they think they will lose all the money they've worked hard for. Their fears are valid because many people have lost 40 to 50 percent of their money in market crashes. If only they knew they could buy insurance to ensure that doesn't happen.

You can and should buy insurance for one of your most important wealth-building assets—your stock market portfolio. But many people don't, and it's not because of cost—stock insurance is often cheaper than car insurance! I believe it's because of misinformation or a lack of information. People don't know that buying insurance for their stock market portfolio is possible. Maybe it's because the insurance has a silly name like put options.

If I told a random stranger I bought puts, they probably wouldn't know what I was talking about. However, most people understand the concept of buying insurance for protection against unexpected financial losses. And yes, I'm fully aware that the idea of stock market insurance sounds far-fetched to some people, but it's simply how it works. You buy portfolio insurance if you want protection against a massive loss, and you sell this type of insurance if you wish to earn income. We'll cover selling put options in the next chapter, but "buying" puts are why I never worry about purchasing stocks at all-time highs.

If I'm worried about the stock crashing, I buy a put option to protect my investment. Purchasing puts is similar to buying insurance to cover the value of my car. I pay a fee or premium for peace of mind that if my vehicle is damaged, the insurance company will give me money to fix it or buy a new car. In the same way, if you have a stock or index fund portfolio, you can buy enough put options to cover its value.

A quick definition of an index before we move on: Unlike a single stock, an index measures the price performance of a basket of securities intended to represent a specific market section. For example, the S&P 500 is an index that tracks the performance of 500 of the largest publicly traded companies in the United States. The index is commonly used as a benchmark for the US stock market. Finally, you cannot directly invest in the S&P 500 index because it does not hold the securities; it just measures the performance of the companies.

The only way to invest in the S&P 500 companies is through index funds and exchange-traded funds (ETFs). As explained in my second book, I no longer buy individual stocks. I'm an index fund investor, and most of our money is in the S&P 500 via SPY (often pronounced as "S.P.Y." or simply "spy"). The ETF SPY owns the stocks included in the S&P 500 index. So when you buy SPY, it's like buying an apartment building with 500 individual units.

Before we move on to a real-life example of an SPY put I bought in my account, let me clarify something. Throughout this book, I will frequently use the term stock insurance, but strictly speaking, there is no such thing as stock insurance. However, put options act as a form of insurance. Here's an example of a put I bought to insure shares of an ETF I purchased: BOUGHT +1 SPY 19 DECEMBER 2025 470 PUT @ $56.50.

STOCK OPTIONS SIMPLIFIED | 41

- **BOUGHT +1** means I bought one contract. If it were -1, I would have sold one contract.
- This is an option contract for the stock symbol **SPY**.
- The contract and its rights are valid until **December 19, 2025.**
- **470** is the "strike price" of the **PUT**. Buying a put gives me the right to "sell" 100 shares of the ETF.

If I exercised the rights of this December 470 put, I could "sell" 100 shares of SPY for $470 a share. I can do this anytime, but I have until December 2025 to exercise these rights. The cost of this insurance was **$56.50** or $5,650, which is called the **options premium**. This is an excellent time to mention that one stock option contract equals 100 shares of a company's stock. So, when you buy one option contract, you purchase the right to buy (calls) or sell (puts) 100 shares of that stock. That's why **any quoted options price you see needs to be multiplied by 100 to determine its actual cost.**

Buying a Call (a.k.a. Long a Call)	Buying a Put (a.k.a. Long a Put)
Right to <u>buy</u> 100 shares of stock.	Right to <u>sell</u> 100 shares of stock.

Table 1: Summary of buying a call and a put option.

One last bit of information about option contracts: If you own a put or call option, you don't have to buy or sell the stock if you don't want to. If you don't exercise the rights of your option contract or close it by the expiration date, you lose the money paid for it. In other words, option contracts give you the right (or option) to buy or sell a stock at a specific price for a limited time. After this period, your contract expires worthless with no value, and your option ceases to exist.

I want to conclude this chapter by returning to my earlier statement about how anyone with basic common sense can understand options. Was I correct? Did you understand this chapter? I'm not asking if you know "how" to buy calls or puts. Even if the information was new to you, did you comprehend what I said about putting small down payments on stocks you want to purchase or buying market crash insurance for your stocks? If I completely lost you, no worries. Just keep learning about options; you'll eventually understand them. However, if you did understand what I said, congratulations—you currently have the mental capacity to understand and succeed with options.

In conclusion, options are insurance contracts that protect you from losing money in the stock market. However, if options protect you, why do so many people say options are risky? It's because they haven't been adequately educated on how options work. The good news is that you have this book to learn a low-risk and prudent way of using options. It's simple: You can buy put options for protection, or as you'll see in the next chapter, you can earn income by selling put insurance to other investors.

3

BUFFETT'S SECRET STRATEGY

SELLING PUT OPTIONS

> *Those who stay in a job they hate are doubly penalized. Not only do they despise their work, but worse yet, it doesn't even make them wealthy ... they waste their lives and their chances of becoming truly rich by clinging to a type of security that is mediocre at best.*
>
> — MARK FISHER

M ost people view Warren Buffett as a stock investor and assume he accumulated wealth by buying businesses. But many don't know that he also uses a secret options strategy that has generated billions in profit over the years. His use of options is rarely talked about. I've only seen a handful of articles discussing one of his most profitable strategies, selling put options for income (Baldwin 2012). Before we get to that, let me explain why we are covering Buffett's strategy.

As stated in an earlier chapter, the book will focus on teaching an income-generating strategy called a put credit spread. It's a two-part strategy that can be confusing because it combines buying and selling options. So, to help you understand credit spreads better, I'm teaching the concepts of buying and selling options separately. Then, later on, I will bring it all together. Thus far, we've already covered one part of the credit spread trade: buying options for protection. Now, we will explore the selling side, as selling put options is how you generate the income portion of the credit spread.

Let's quickly recap the buying of puts, and then we will focus on the selling side of the transaction. Remember, stock options are nothing but contracts. Whether it's an option contract or a real estate contract, there are always two parties to each transaction: the buyer (who pays money for the benefit of the contract) and the seller (who receives money for providing the benefit). When you purchase a put option, you essentially buy market crash protection.

- The buyer of a put option has the **right to sell** 100 shares of a stock at a fixed price. Again, this fixed price is known as the exercise or strike price of the put. If the stock fell in price, you could file an insurance claim to recover your money. This is called exercising your put option.

Let's now talk about the person who sold you the put option. Well, buying and selling puts are opposites. If you understand one side of the transaction, you can reverse it to understand the other side.

- The <u>seller of a put option</u> created an **obligation to buy** 100 shares of a stock at a fixed price. Also, this obligation is in effect until the expiration date of the options contract. However, it's a potential obligation because you will only have to buy the stock if the purchaser of the put decides to exercise their rights.

Remember, this is an insurance transaction. It's a contract in which, in exchange for a fee, one party agrees to compensate another party in the event of a loss. But why would someone put themselves in a position to "have to" buy stock? Well, for one, some people are okay with purchasing additional shares of stock. Getting paid to do so is simply a bonus.

It can also be highly profitable. Put-sellers get paid to take on this "potential" risk, and in most cases, they keep the income without buying the stock. It's no different from car or home insurance. My insurance company makes money by promising me a benefit. They will only pay if I file an insurance claim. Since I've never had to file one, they have pocketed all the premiums I paid them over the years. Now, let's review how Warren Buffett makes money with stock insurance.

GETTING PAID TO BUY STOCKS: A MILLION-DOLLAR PUT SELLING EXAMPLE

In the previous chapter, we pretended you had bought insurance to protect your 100 shares of stock XYZ. We will now focus on the other side of that transaction, the person who sold you the insurance. To demonstrate, I'll use a trade Warren Buffett himself placed. The following is just one of many instances where Buffett used options in his overall investment strategy.

In 1993, Warren Buffett, known for his bargain hunting, had his eyes on more Coca-Cola stock. However, he wasn't willing to pay the current market price. Instead of passively waiting for the stock price to drop, he used a unique "paid-to-wait" approach to options. He sold put options at the price he was willing to pay for the stock—roughly 10 percent lower than where it was trading. In other words, some investor(s) wanted insurance for their stock in case it fell in price, so they bought put options. Buffett sold the puts, thus agreeing to buy the stock if it fell in price. In exchange for selling the puts and taking on the potential stock purchase risk, Buffett received $7.5 million in income (InvestorPlace 2017).

The investor(s) who own shares of Coca-Cola have the assurance that if the stock drops by 10 percent, they can exercise their put insurance contract and recover their investment losses. Buffett is on the other end of this insurance contract, patiently waiting for the stock to fall roughly 10 percent in price. It's brilliant if you ask me. Buffett was paid 7.5 million dollars to buy stock at a 10 percent discount. There are only two scenarios that could have played out for him:

1. If Coca-Cola's stock fell below the puts strike price before the option contracts expired, the buyers of the options may exercise those puts and sell their shares to Buffett. This is precisely what he wanted to do in the first place: buy the shares at a discounted price. The money earned from selling the puts helps finance a portion of the stock purchase.

2. Alternatively, if Coca-Cola's stock rose in price, the owners of the put option contract would not exercise their insurance. There's no reason to file an insurance claim if the stock didn't crash in price. So, like all unused insurance, the contracts would expire, and Buffett would pocket the $7.5 million in premium income. This outcome demonstrates the profit potential even when the stock price doesn't fall.

Buffett could have avoided options and waited for Coca-Cola's price to fall, which is what most investors do. But he took a much superior approach, being paid millions to buy a stock he already wanted to buy. He created a unique win-win scenario: He buys a quality stock at a discounted price or pockets the income from selling put options. It's simple: You sell put options on stocks you want to own, and you will either buy the stock or you won't. Either way, you keep the premium received.

I wanted to share Buffett's insurance trade so that you get a big-picture overview of selling put options. Understanding the concept of selling puts is vital because it's one of the two parts of the credit spread strategy. Regardless, selling stock insurance to other investors is a great way to earn passive income. You sell the insurance, and then you sit and wait. No physical work is required. Buffett didn't have to work for the $7.5 million. He merely offered a benefit to someone. The great news is that any investor, not just billionaires, can sell puts this way.

An Important Fact About Selling Put Options

Let me show you one of the put-selling trades I made in my retirement account. My profits are much more modest since I'm not a billionaire like Buffett.

01/25/2024	Sell to Open	SPY 03/01/2024 487.00 P	2	$5.69	$1.34	$1,136.66
	Trade Details	PUT SPDR S&P 500 $487				
		EXP 03/01/24				

Figure 2: An example of selling a put option on SPY, Source: Schwab.com

The put trade, shown in Figure 2, brought in $1,136 in income—money that was immediately deposited into my account once I placed the trade. It's mine to keep whether I buy the stock or not. I opened several of these trades in 2024. Since the market rose in price, none of the insurance contracts were exercised because the buyers didn't need the insurance. This means I kept the premium without being forced to buy stock. In other words, I make money as long as I don't have to pay out an insurance claim, and the only thing that will cause me to pay out a claim is the stock falling in price.

That simple process can be repeated for years to come. And yes, the stock will eventually fall, and I'll have to buy it. But that's okay—I'll enjoy the passive income while I wait. Now, imagine for a moment that you could do this each month. Wouldn't it feel good to click a few buttons and bring in thousands in instant income? Well, I can confirm that it does feel good, and my goal is to help you earn thousands or more each month.

And now that I have tickled your greed gland, I want to share the dirty little secret of the put-selling community. Gurus will entice you with the allure of swimming in dollar bills each month. However, an important fact you probably won't find mentioned on the sales page of a put-selling course is this: Selling put options, like Buffett, requires a lot of money in your account. In my case, the broker would lock up $97,400 (487 strike price × 200 shares). They would make that amount unavailable for other investments. This is what is known as a **margin requirement**. Sure, you can find a lower-priced stock to sell puts on, but in doing so, you also lower the income you receive.

With that in mind, let's dig further into my SPY put trade. I sold two 487-strike put options on SPY. Someone wanted insurance for their SPY shares, and I sold it to them. The buyer of the put transferred the risk of loss to me, the seller of the contract. In exchange for taking on that risk, I was paid a cash premium of $5.69 or $569 per contract sold. Excluding commissions, I brought in $1,138 in income, but the insurance policy I sold comes with significant risk!

Let's pretend the stock crashed in price to $200. The buyer of the puts would exercise their options (i.e., file an insurance claim). I would then be forced to buy 200 shares from them at the agreed-upon price of $487. This is equivalent to paying out an insurance claim that cost me $97,400. Now you see why the broker locks up my cash as a margin requirement. With this transaction, I risk losing nearly one hundred grand in exchange for a thousand-dollar profit.

Also, the initial premium deposited into my account when I sold the put is the most I can make. So, as you can see, selling a put involves considerable risk and limited profit potential. This is the sobering truth about selling puts that's rarely talked about. Everyone brags about the passive income, but you never hear about anyone getting wealthy from selling put options. Think about it: If selling puts was an excellent way to grow your money, wouldn't people like Buffett devote all their resources to it? Selling put options is fantastic for earning income on idle cash, but it's a horrible strategy for growing your money. In my experience, buying and holding the S&P 500 outperforms a put-selling strategy.

Now that you know those ugly truths, how enticing does selling puts seem now? Regardless, this is precisely what many investors do from their home computers or mobile phones. They sell put options and create another income source without getting a second job. Anyone can start one of these stock insurance companies. You can sell these contracts as long as you have the money to satisfy the obligation of the put you sold.

Stock Insurance Recap

The option nerds like to make this more complicated than it needs to be, but it's simple in principle. You buy put options for protection, and you sell put options for income. Keep that simple overview in mind because, in the next chapter, you'll discover how to combine these benefits to create a third strategy called a put credit spread. It has a weird name, but it will make sense once I explain it. Credit spreads are a more conservative income generation strategy than selling single puts. For example, with a credit spread, you could have brought in $1,170 in income, and the margin requirement needed to place the trade would only be $3,000. That's much better than needing $97,400. All of this and more will be shown in the next few chapters. I can't wait to share it with you!

Buying a Put (a.k.a.) Long a Put	Selling a Put (a.k.a.) Short a Put
Right to sell 100 shares of stock.	Obligation to buy 100 shares of stock.
It makes money if stocks fall in price.	It makes money if stocks rise in price.
Loses money if stocks rise in price.	Loses money if stocks fall in price.

Table 2: A summary of buying and selling put options

4

INTRO TO PUT CREDIT SPREADS

> *If you don't find a way to make money while you sleep, you will work until you die.*
>
> — WARREN BUFFETT

We're finally here—the book's core strategy for earning consistent monthly income. Yes, we took the long scenic route to get here, but it was essential for those who are newer to options and the benefits they provide to investors. Nonetheless, at this point, you understand that people buy put options to protect their investment portfolios, and others sell put options to earn income from offering that insurance. Now it's time to reveal how to combine these two strategies to create a third strategy called a put credit spread. It's a low-risk insurance trade that makes money while you sleep because it profits from the passing of time without incident (more on this later).

When you employ this strategy, you'll no longer have to trade time for dollars like at a corporate job. And since it's not a day trading strategy, you won't have to be tied to your computer desk all day. However, please understand that this is not a get-rich-quick strategy. It's a passive income strategy that takes patience, prudence, and discipline to succeed with it.

Before we begin, a quick note. I frequently refer to credit spreads as the cash flow trade because they generate consistent income for us. Another reason I like that term is because I dislike the technical jargon that Wall Street uses. I believe these so-called experts intentionally try to complicate investing because if you are confused, you'll feel insecure about your ability to manage your own money. And, of course, they will be standing by, ready and willing to manage it for you, getting paid a commission whether you make money or not. Anyhoo, enough of my conspiracy theories—let's return to the lesson.

MAKING BUFFETT'S INSURANCE TRADE LESS RISKY

Warren Buffett has made billions from using options in a particular way, and by modeling his approach, we, too, can profit from selling stock insurance. However, there's a tweak you can make to the put-selling strategy to transform it into a more conservative trade called a put credit spread. This tweak lowers the cash requirement and risk of loss, but it can still generate the same income. It's only two simple steps, both of which you learned about earlier in the book. I will use my put trade, which is shown in the last chapter, to demonstrate.

Step 1: SOLD -2 SPY 1 MARCH 2024 487 PUT @ $5.69 (I sold stock insurance to an investor, similar to Buffett's million-dollar trade).

This put generated $1,138 in income ($5.69 × 200). If I'm forced to buy the stock (i.e., pay out an insurance claim), I'll need $97,400 to buy 200 shares of SPY at $487 a share. However, you can tweak this insurance trade to bring in roughly the same amount of money and dramatically reduce your risk of loss. For example, you can bring in $1,170 in income, but the risk of loss will only be $1,830. It's yet another concept I learned from Warren Buffett. We've already discussed how he sells insurance, but if you read Berkshire Hathaway's shareholder reports, you will discover they also own a reinsurance company. And that's what we will use with this put trade; we will buy reinsurance.

Reinsurance is insurance for people who sell insurance. It transfers risk to another entity to reduce the likelihood of large insurance claim payouts. Put more simply, insurance companies buy their own insurance to limit how much they can lose if they pay out a claim. And that's the slight tweak we will make to this put trade. With credit spreads, you are an insurance seller <u>and</u> an insurance buyer.

Step 2: BOUGHT +2 SPY 1 MARCH 2024 482 PUT @ $3.74 (I bought an insurance policy to protect myself from the massive risk of selling the other put).

I did not place this second step in real life, but this is what I would have done to transform my riskier put trade into a more conservative credit spread trade. I would have bought a put option with a lower strike price, <u>which cost less</u> than the put I sold (the slight tweak). In Step 1, I sell two insurance policies to someone and receive an instant deposit of $1,138 into my account (excluding commissions and fees). In Step 2, I take a portion of my income and buy two insurance policies for $748 ($3.74 × 200). This second step of purchasing reinsurance reduces my cash requirement and the risk of loss. Afterward, I am left with a credit of $390. <u>This $390 is my potential max profit as long as I don't have to pay any insurance claims</u> (i.e., buy stock shares).

Summary: I'm selling insurance to an investor and buying an insurance policy to protect myself from a massive loss. These are two separate transactions that are <u>opened simultaneously as a pair</u>. With the second part of the spread (buying the put), I am reducing how much money I potentially have to pay someone. Also, the broker sees I'm buying reinsurance, so they lower this trade's cash or margin requirement from $97,400 to $1,000. That lower margin requirement represents the $1,000 risk between those two put trades. If the stock crashed in price and the put I sold was exercised, I'd have to buy $97,400 worth of stock. However, I can sell the same shares for $96,400 if I exercise the put I purchased.

There you have it—that's the risk-reducing tweak we can make to Buffett's cash-intensive insurance trade. This tweak is traditionally known as a credit spread trade. Since the put you sell is responsible for the credit, it's considered "selling" a put credit spread.

Why It's Called a Put Credit Spread

It's finally time to explain the strategy's geeky name. First, this strategy or trade is constructed using put options, not call options. Second, after you implement these two put transactions, there's a credit left over, which is immediately deposited into your account. Think bank accounts: Debits are when money leaves your account, and credits are when money is deposited into your account. Finally, there is a price spread between the strike or exercise prices of the two put trades.

Now that the option terminology has been explained, I want to address a common concern people raise when learning this strategy. At least one person thinks, *Hold up, Travis. We just went from a potential profit of $1,138 with the single puts to a potential profit of $390 with the credit spread. I'd say your little tweak sucks!* Well, if that's what you're thinking, smarty-pants, here is an easy fix. Just sell and buy more insurance contacts. If I sold six of these put credit spreads, the cash margin requirement would be $3,000, and here is what the transaction would look like:

- **Step 1:** Sell 6 SPY 487 puts for a credit of $5.69 per contract.
- **Step 2:** Buy 6 SPY 482 puts for a debit of $3.74 per contract.
- $5.69 - $3.74 = $1.95 (Remember, this figure needs to be multiplied by 100).

The ending credit of $195 × 6 contracts = $1,170 in potential profit with a maximum possible loss of only $1,830. And if you're wondering how you determine the maximum loss of the credit spread or the margin requirement, we will cover that in the next chapter. Also, to calculate the percent return, you divide the potential profit by the potential loss. If the trade works out, it's a 64 percent return on the risk. This is much better than selling the single puts because that only produced a 1.2 percent return on the $97K margin requirement. Finally, a credit spread is a defined risk strategy; how much you can make and lose is a fixed amount.

Here's a little encouragement before we move on. Please don't let the math and nuances of the strategy discourage you or cause you to miss the overall point. Credit spreads give you the best of both worlds; they provide income and protection against a massive loss. With the credit spread, I reduced my risk of loss and increased my return on cash. And that process, compounded over time, is how you build massive wealth. Another way of looking at this is that the strategy gives you a lower-risk way of participating in the highly profitable insurance business. Think about it: Don't insurance companies bring in billions in passive income each year? And how often does the average person file an insurance claim?

I'll use my life as an example. We have four insurance policies with a local agent. We have not spoken to him since he sold us the policies twelve years ago. However, we occasionally get letters from his agency notifying us that our insurance premiums are increasing. Stated more sarcastically, we get letters informing us that his monthly profit is rising, with no extra work done on his end. Part of me is annoyed by this, and part of me is envious, but it's the deal we made with him. He generates passive income from us each year to provide peace of mind and ensure that we are protected against unexpected financial losses.

The good news is that thanks to credit spreads, you get to join him on the passive income train. But instead of selling home or auto insurance, you will sell stock insurance. As a seller of insurance, you will receive money upfront via premiums, and each day that passes without incident means you will get to keep more of that premium. After a set time, the insurance policy expires, and all that money paid to you is yours to keep. In summary, **insurance policies profit from the passing of time without incident.**

The "incident" with put credit spreads is the stock falling in price well below the strike price of the insurance put you sold. This is usually when stock assignment occurs, and you are forced to buy the stock shares. Even though a put credit spread has built-in insurance, there is still the risk of buying stock shares because of the put you sell. Being forced to purchase hundreds of stock shares when you don't want them is a significant hassle. The good news is that there is a way to earn income from credit spreads while eliminating the stock purchase risk and the worry that comes with it. We'll discuss that in the next chapter, but first, let's talk about the two types of credit spreads.

THE TWO TYPES OF CREDIT SPREAD TRADES

Thus far, we've only talked about the put credit spread trade, but there are two types. One is best suited for when stocks are going up in price, and the other is best suited for when stocks fall in price. And in certain situations, they both allow you to make money with stocks that go nowhere in price (stagnant stocks). Now, let me ask: If you have a tool in your investing toolbox that allows you to make money in any economic environment, is there a need to worry about the direction of the stock market? I don't think so, but I'm biased because I've been trading options for over twenty-five years and through all kinds of craziness.

Bullish and Bearish Credit Spreads

- A **bullish credit spread** is constructed using put options and enables you to make money when stocks trade sideways or rise in price.
- A **bearish credit spread** is constructed using call options and enables you to make money when stocks trade sideways or fall in price.

In general terms, bullish means you think a stock or the overall market is heading higher, and bearish means you believe a stock or the market is heading lower in price. These two strategies are often called bull put spreads and bear call spreads; however, I rarely use those terms as they confuse new traders. Most new traders associate puts with stocks going down in price, so having the bull in the name throws people off. Vice versa with the bear call spread. Thus, I usually call them put credit spreads or call credit spreads.

Before we dig deeper, here is a bit of disappointing news. From now on, I will only focus on the put credit spread. Historically, the market goes up more than it goes down, so the bullish credit spread is the one you'll use 80 to 90 percent of the time. That's why I consider it your core cash flow trade. The good news is that once you master the bullish credit spread, it's easier to understand the bearish credit spread because they are the opposite of each other. If you know one of the spreads, you can reverse the mechanics to understand the other spread trade.

Stock and Index Spreads

In addition to the bullish and bearish credit spreads, you also have stock and index spreads. The credit spreads we have discussed thus far are stock spreads and can be sold on any stock that has listed options. However, we won't use stock options for the credit spread strategy; we'll sell index credit spreads. The next chapter will discuss the differences between stock and index options. However, let me quickly share an example of selling a put on SPX, the ticker symbol for the S&P 500 index options:

- SOLD -1 SPX, 18 OCT 2024 4900 PUT for $173.70

Can you see the difference between puts on stocks and indexes? Let me point it out: If you recall from an earlier example, I sold SPY puts and generated $1,138 in instant income. If I had sold the above SPX put on the index, I would have had $17,370 deposited into my account (again, the $173.70 option price needs to be multiplied by

100). That sounds fantastic until you realize that selling that 4900 put option represents 100 index shares. In other words, it would require nearly half a million dollars in your account for each put you sell.

Most of my clients invest within their retirement accounts, and when you sell puts inside a retirement account, the broker requires you to have the total amount needed if the put is exercised. In this case, the broker would lock up $490,000 for the margin requirement, making the money unavailable for other purposes. The rules for taxable accounts differ a bit, but they are beyond the scope of this book because we aren't focused on selling puts for income. Instead, we will sell credit spreads, which require much less money.

Finally, I know these examples are out of reach for most people, but that doesn't mean we can't learn from them and model them on a smaller scale. And as you will soon see, that's precisely what I did with my credit spread trades. Selling index options is a great way to earn income from puts, but you never have to worry about buying a stock. This is yet another put-selling approach Warren Buffett used, but this approach earned him billions in profit. We'll talk about this and more in the next chapter. See you there!

5

BUFFETT'S BILLION-DOLLAR
INCOME TRADE

> *If you want to achieve success, all you need to do is find a way to model those who have already succeeded.*
>
> — TONY ROBBINS

Thus far, we have only covered "stock" options, and if you sell put options on individual stocks, it's best to take Warren Buffett's approach: Use the strategy to get paid to buy stocks at discounted prices. However, we have one more Buffett option trade to cover that aligns more with our strategy of selling credit spreads. In addition to selling put options on stocks, Buffett also earned billions in profit from selling puts on indices. Between 2004 and 2007, Buffett sold $4.5 billion worth of put options on the S&P 500 and three other indices. He sold an additional

$400 million worth of puts in 2008, putting the total premium received at $4.9 billion (Chow 2024).

When Buffett sold those puts, he was betting that the future price of the index would be higher. If he was correct, he kept the billions in put premiums received. If he were wrong, he would have lost billions. However, the big difference with this put trade is that, unlike stock options, index options have no stock assignment risk. That's why we won't use stock options for the credit spread strategy; we'll use index options.

STOCK OPTIONS VERSUS INDEX OPTIONS

Since I no longer buy individual stocks but am an index fund investor, I will only discuss the difference between SPY and SPX, stock symbols representing the S&P 500. For all practical purposes, SPY and SPX are the same, and **you can trade options on both**. The big difference is that SPY is an ETF, and you can buy shares. SPX represents the index itself, and you can't buy shares of an index.

- When you purchase a SPY option contract, you have the right (but not the obligation) to buy or sell **100 shares** of that stock. Stock and ETF options are what you call American-style. This means they can be exercised at any time before expiration.

- When you <u>purchase</u> an SPX option contract, you have the right (but not the obligation) to buy or sell the **cash value** of the S&P 500 at a specified strike price. The difference between the options' strike price and the index value is exchanged in cash. For example, if you buy an SPX 3,000 put option and the index expires at 2,900, you have a $100 profit with the put. The $100 profit × 100 shares means you will be paid $10,000 cash rather than selling 100 shares at 3,000. Also, index options are European style. This means they can only be exercised at expiration.

Before I further explain why we use index options for the credit spread, let me quickly explain why someone might buy an index option instead of a stock option. Investors worried about the economy might purchase insurance on an index rather than a specific stock. Roughly 70 to 80 percent of individual stocks trend in the same direction as the S&P. So instead of buying a put for each stock they own, which would be expensive, they buy a put on the index itself. So people like Buffett, who have large sums of money, gladly sell this insurance to other investors. However, we are only interested in index options because of how the assignment is handled.

Why I Sell Index Spreads and Not Stock Spreads

Credit spreads can be implemented on any stock that has listed options. However, I will strongly discourage you from selling spreads on individual stocks because of the stock assignment risk. Assignment is the process that describes what happens when the rights of an option contract are exercised. When a stock option is exercised, stock shares are exchanged. When an index option is exercised, the assignment is settled in cash payments since you can't own or purchase index shares. Remember, an index measures the performance of the companies; it doesn't hold the securities.

How an assignment is handled seems like a small detail, but it makes a huge difference when selling credit spreads. Let's compare an SPY and SPX spread to see the big difference.

- Step 1: Sell -2 SPY 18 OCT 2024 487 PUT @ $5.69
- Step 2: Buy +2 SPY 18 OCT 2024 482 PUT @ $3.74

Remember, a credit spread involves selling a put and then simultaneously buying a put to protect you. Step 1 is the main engine of the credit spread. All the profit (and risk of loss) originates from the put you sold. Thus, the put credit spread makes money when stocks rise, loses money if stocks fall in price, and carries assignment risk if the stock stays below the put you sold.

If you sell a put credit spread on a "stock" and the put you sold is <u>exercised</u>, you will be assigned (or must buy) stock shares. Remember, with stock options, assignment can happen at any time; however, it usually occurs when the stock trades well below the put's strike price. If the assignment never occurs, you keep the income received from selling the credit spread.

Experienced credit spread traders always point out that the stock assignment risk can be managed by manually closing the trade if it's losing money. They also discuss the put you bought, the spread's built-in market crash protection, and how you can exercise it if you are forced to buy stock. Those are great points, but stocks rarely crash in price at convenient times, and why create more work for yourself when you don't have to? You could be on vacation or at work and get exercised, and then you'll get margin calls from your broker. It's a terrifying experience for most, as the broker demands you deposit large sums of money into your account within a few days.

In some cases, like what happened to me, the broker's risk department went into my account and started closing trades without notifying me. They didn't even give me a chance to deal with the assignment. In other words, selling credit spreads on stocks requires constant monitoring because assignments can happen any time before the options expire. They must be continuously managed until the spreads are closed. Is that the kind of stress and hassle you want in your life? I don't. I avoid that inconvenience by only selling spreads with index options because the assignment is settled in cash. Let's walk through that process.

Intro to the SPX Put Credit Spread

By using index options like Buffett, you can eliminate the stock purchase risk and the worry that comes with it. When you sell an SPX credit spread, only two things can happen: You will make or lose money. You get the income without the stock assignment risk. Any money you made or lost from your spread is added to or removed from your trading account. No index shares are bought or sold. Here is what a comparable SPX put credit spread would look like. Again, Step 1 is the credit spread's core profit and loss engine.

- Step 1: Sell -2 SPX, 18 OCT 2024 4900 put @ $173.70 per contract
- Step 2: Buy +2 SPX, 18 OCT 2024 4875 put @ $166.45 per contract
- $173.70 - $166.45 = $7.25
- The ending credit of $725 × 2 contracts = $1,450 in potential profit

When you sell credit spreads on SPX, you will make money if the price of the S&P 500 stays above the strike prices of the spread you sold, and you'll lose money if it doesn't. Also, with an "index" option, an assignment can only occur on expiration day and would happen if SPX is below your puts strike price. If the option is <u>exercised</u>, there are no shares to buy; you would instead deliver a cash payment to the put buyer. If the assignment never occurs, you keep the income received from selling the credit spread. In summary, SPX credit spreads are easier to manage and less hassle than selling spreads on individual stocks. If the index crashes in price after you open the spread, you don't have to worry about it. There will be no assignment until the spread's expiration date.

Finally, they have a slightly better tax treatment. Broad-based index options are taxed according to the 60/40 rule: 60 percent of the profit is treated as long-term gains and 40 percent as short-term gains, regardless of the holding period. However, tax laws may change over time. Please consult a qualified tax advisor to understand how your specific options trades will be taxed, especially if you're trading in a taxable account. For instance, my accountant suggested I close the SPX spreads in my taxable account at year-end because I'm taxed on my open trades even though I haven't booked the profit. Then, I can re-open them the following year or start a new batch of spreads to sell. Again, talk to an accountant; I'm not a tax expert.

SPX (Index) Options	SPY (ETF) Options
Can Only be Exercised at Expiration	Can be Exercised at Any Time
Section 1256 Tax Benefits (60/40)	Standard Tax Treatment
Cash-Settled	Settled with Stock Shares

Table 3: Comparison of SPX and SPY options.

With SPX credit spreads, there are only two outcomes—
not a gazillion, just two: You'll either make or lose money.
And you know precisely how much you can make or lose
before you sell the credit spread. Since index options can't
be assigned early, any stock movement between the time
you place the trade and the day the options expire is irrel-
evant to the outcome of the trade. The only thing that
matters is the price of the S&P 500 on the spread's expiration day.

- You will make money if, on expiration day, the
  price of the S&P 500 is above the strike prices of
  the spread you sold.
- If the stock crashes in price after you open the
  spread and never recovers, you don't have to
  worry about buying stock shares. You'll lose
  money, and the loss will be deducted from your
  account at the spread's expiration.
- In rare situations, the SPX option will expire
  below the put you sold (which will be exercised)

BUFFETT'S BILLION-DOLLAR INCOME TRADE | 75

but above the protection put you bought (which expires worthless). It's scary but nothing to concern yourself with because the trade is cash-settled. The broker will close the trade, and you'll incur a relatively small loss, which will be debited from your account. It will be the difference between the options' strike price and the index's price.

Either way, the stock market's performance is out of your control, so there's no need to stress about the results. Embrace the uncertainty of the stock market and focus on what you can control: your risk of loss, etc. Speaking of losses, let's cover how to figure that out.

Determining the Max Loss and Margin Requirement

If you hate math, brace yourself. I have a short math lesson to teach you how to determine the maximum loss and margin requirement of the SPX credit spread we just reviewed.

Margin Requirement Calculation

- Calculate the difference between the spread's strike prices: $4900 - $4875 = $25, or $2,500, since the price needs to be multiplied by 100.

- Then, multiply this figure by the number of contracts you sold: $2,500 × 2 = a margin requirement of $5,000.

The broker would require this amount to place this particular credit spread in your account. Of course, this amount will change depending on the spread you sell.

Max Loss Calculation

- Calculate the difference between the spread's strike prices: $4900 - $4875 = $2,500.
- Then, subtract the credit you received from the above figure: $2,500 - $725 = $1,775. This is how much you can lose for each contract you sell.
- Next, multiply $1,775 by the number of contracts you sold: $1,775 × 2 = a potential loss of $3,550. If your SPX spread loses money, the broker removes this amount from your account when the spread expires.

That's a lot of math, but here's the good news: Most brokers will display the maximum profit and loss figures when you place the trade, so you don't have to calculate it manually. However, if they don't, it's still good for you to know how to calculate it manually yourself.

Also, the great thing about index credit spreads is that they are genuinely defined risk strategies. You cannot make more than the maximum profit, but, more importantly, you cannot lose more than the maximum loss. Credit spreads on stocks start as a defined risk strategy, but if you are assigned stock shares, it's no longer a credit spread trade. At that point, it can turn into a multi-thousand-dollar nightmare. Yeah, no thanks; I've been there and done that and no longer want that type of stress.

Before we move on to the next chapter, let's quickly review what you have learned thus far. You discovered that credit spreads give average investors a low-risk way to participate in the same insurance business as Buffett: collecting premiums to insure people against market crashes. However, as you discovered, selling put options like Buffet is very cash-intensive. I don't know about you, but where I'm from, the average person doesn't have an extra $490,000 lying around. This is why we are profiling the put credit spread, a risk-reducing strategy.

With credit spreads, you profit from selling insurance to other investors but then take a portion of your income and buy a reinsurance policy. The reinsurance purchased as part of the spread reduces the risk of selling single puts while still allowing us to earn a decent income. It's a strategic way to get income from selling put options without the massive risk and cash requirement of selling single puts. The downfall of the credit spread is that it lowers your potential profit, but selling more contracts solves this issue. You also discovered that with index credit spreads, there is no stock assignment risk; you only manage profits and losses.

In summary, the put credit spread is a lower-risk way to sell puts but is still a stock insurance trade at its core. You lose money if a disaster strikes (stocks fall in price), and you make money if no disaster strikes (stocks rise or trade sideways in price). Of course, learning all the details of the credit spread can be tedious and annoying, but that was a simple summary of the strategy.

Finally, don't let all the math discourage you from learning this strategy. Review the basic concepts repeatedly until you become a pro at making passive income from the stock market. The effort to understand this will be one of the best financial decisions of your life. After you master it, you'll be empowered to make money whether stocks go up, down, or sideways in price. It takes only ten minutes to sell a credit spread, and then you sit on your hands for a few weeks to months and wait for your profit to materialize. Although this strategy is not 100 percent passive, it is low-maintenance. There's also no cap on how much you can make. As your account grows, so will your income.

That said, I want to caution you. When you start placing your first few trades, clicking buttons and having cash instantly deposited into your account will be exciting. But never forget that by clicking those buttons, you are entering into a contractual obligation to provide insurance for someone. You're running a business, not playing a video game, so the risk of loss must always be managed. Never forget that! With that out of the way, let's move on so you can learn how to place these instant income trades yourself.

6

HOW TO OPEN AND CLOSE A PUT CREDIT SPREAD

> *Make your money work for you so that one day, you won't need to work for it.*
>
> — PAULA PANT

This chapter aims to familiarize you with opening and closing spreads so you are less overwhelmed when you do it in real life. It's not meant to turn you into a pro at opening spreads. Ultimately, practicing on a broker's platform is the best way to learn how to open and close credit spreads. And most brokers have tutorials to show you how to use their platform.

Despite the tutorials, selling your first credit spread can still be intimidating. I compare the experience to learning how to drive a car. It was initially terrifying, and I thought I'd never get the hang of driving. But over time and with practice, I got better. Now, it's easy to do. Learning how to trade credit spreads is a similar learning experience.

It's common for people to get overwhelmed when they log into a brokerage account to sell a credit spread. If that happens, I want you to take a deep breath and focus on the simple principles of your actions. **You are learning to generate passive income from selling stock insurance to other investors.** Don't stress yourself out or let negative self-talk get in the way of a brighter future. It's a new concept and will take time to understand, but you only need to learn it once. That being said, let's discuss the type of brokerage account you will need for this strategy.

WHAT TYPE OF ACCOUNT WILL YOU NEED?

If you don't have a brokerage account, you'll want to search online for "options trading brokers." Several reputable firms exist. I would list them here, but brokerages are constantly changing. With technological advances, opening a brokerage account is a relatively simple process. Nowadays, they have tutorials to walk you through it, and if you get stuck, you can always call their customer support and have someone guide you through the process.

You'll likely need to deposit at least $2,500 or more to open a brokerage account, which is technically enough to start trading options. However, I always encourage people to begin with at least $5,000 to $10,000. You will make mistakes, so you need enough money to survive them. If you already have a brokerage account where you invest, you can contact them to see if they allow options trading.

Approval levels differ among brokers, but you want to **look for an options approval level that allows you to trade spreads.** The great news is that these can also be traded inside most individual retirement accounts. If you get denied for trading credit spreads, it's not uncommon. Most people consider options risky, so some prominent brokers want to ensure you have enough experience. If denied, or you don't get approved for the level you want, wait three to six months and apply again. While you wait, you can practice the strategy on paper or virtual trade (more on this in the template chapter). Now, let's cover how you would place a put credit spread trade and a few things to watch out for.

SELLING A PUT CREDIT SPREAD

For reference, option-selling strategies produce credits in your account, and option-buying strategies create debits in your account. Since money will be deposited to your account when you open a put credit spread, it's considered "selling" a spread. In reality, you open two individual puts trades simultaneously, but the pair is viewed as a credit spread. You sell the pair of options to open a credit spread. Let me pull up an example SPX credit spread, and then I'll walk you through how I would open this trade.

- **Trade #1:** Sell to Open 5 SPX, 17 APR 2025 5860 PUT for $190.15 (the income trade).
- **Trade #2:** Buy to Open 5 SPX, 17 APR 2025 5850 PUT for $187.30 (the protection trade).
- The ending credit per spread sold is $2.85, or $285. Since we sold five contracts, the total credit is $1,425.

The bullish spread in the example above was constructed by <u>selling to open</u> a higher premium put trade and then <u>buying to open</u> a lower premium put trade. In other words, the bullish spread is constructed by selling a higher strike put option and buying a lower strike put with the same expiration date. **These are two separate transactions opened simultaneously as a pair.** The two trades should never be separated. If I separate the two above transactions, I will have a different strategy with a different risk and reward.

For instance, if I were to close the 5850 puts by accident, I'd be left with the five 5860 puts I sold. If that happened, the broker would require me to have $2,930,000 in my account to cover the potential put assignment ($5860 × 500). So again, always keep the two put trades together! I repeat, open them together and close them together. Always!

<u>Please note</u>: I will explain how to open these trades in my Charles Schwab broker account. However, broker platforms change over time, so the way to place orders may change. I'm sharing this to show you how simple opening a credit spread trade is. However, simple does not mean it will be easy. When you first learn to place these trades, all the buttons and order options are overwhelming. But it eventually becomes a simple process that even my nine-year-old son can follow.

Is my son a pro at selling credit spreads? No! Can he adequately explain what he's doing? Probably not. But he can follow simple instructions and click what buttons he's told to click. So, even if this is initially overwhelming, give yourself at least six months of practice, and I'm confident you will get the hang of it. One last point: My son and wife don't place these trades off memory. They have step-by-step notes they use. Those notes are similar to the steps you see below. I figured they'd work for you since they work for them as option novices.

Step 1: Once I log in, I click the trade tab, then options. This takes me to where I can type the stock ticker symbol of the instrument on which I want to trade options. In my case, it's generally SPX (the S&P 500). With my other broker, I can type in SPX. However, with Schwab, I have to put a dollar sign in front of SPX.

Step 2: After I enter the ticker symbol, I click the strategy drop-down menu and choose "vertical put" in the two-leg spreads column. Two-leg means there are two separate transactions in the strategy. The term vertical describes the position of the strike prices, one higher and one lower, with the same expiration date. All the other listed strategies can be ignored. They are beyond the scope of this book, and most of them are for people who actively trade, and that's not what I'm teaching you. I'm showing you how to be a passive options investor.

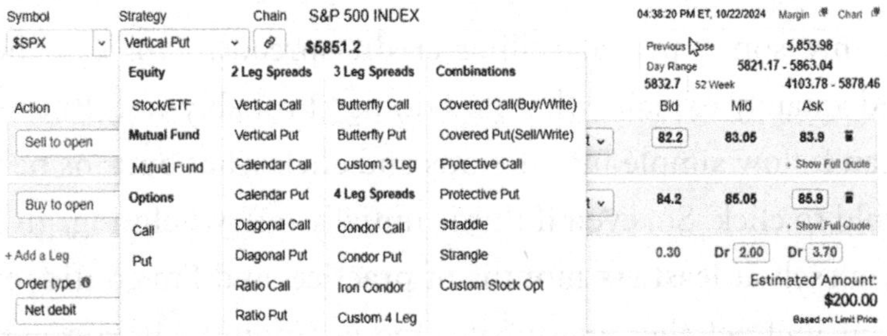

Figure 3: Choosing a vertical put credit spread strategy (Step 2), Source: Schwab.com

Step 3: Once I click "vertical put," the order screen pulls up. There, I focus on three main things: expiration date, strike prices, and number of contracts. I first click the drop-down menu with the option expiration dates and choose the date I want (more on this in a later chapter). Then, I move to the right and ensure the sell-to-open row has the higher strike put option. If that's the case, the net quote row under the option prices should show CR, which indicates I am receiving a credit. If it shows DR, you are about to place a debit spread, which costs money. You don't want that; you want cash flowing into your account, not out of it. Debit spreads are beyond this book's scope, so always ensure you are receiving a credit.

Then, I review the order type at the bottom left of the screen to ensure it says net credit. For the limit price, most brokers want you to sell options at the price in the bid column ($0.90). However, here's an expert tip to get you a little more money: Set the spread limit price at $0.05 less than the mid-price of the spread. The mid-price of the spread in Figure 4 is $2.85, so I'd adjust my limit price to $2.80 and leave the timing as "day," meaning the order is only suitable for today. If the order is not filled by the end of the day, I will return the next day and try to place the trade again.

Figure 4: Order screen for five long-term SPX put credit spreads (Step 3), Source: Schwab.com

Step 4: Once I set my limit price and know how much I'll receive per credit spread, I change the quantity to sell the desired number of spreads. How many spreads I sell is based on how much money I want to put at risk of losing (more on this in the template chapter). In this example, I will receive $280 per spread I sell, so if I sold five of these, I'd receive a total credit of $1,400, and my max potential loss would be $3,600. You already know how to calculate these figures, but if I click the "trade and probability calculator" link under my trade, it will show me the profit and loss figures. Also, I would need $5,000 to place this trade, which the broker would tie up as the cash margin requirement. Unfortunately, the trade and probability calculator section will not show how much money you need to place this credit spread trade in your account. However, we covered margin requirements in the previous chapter.

Figure 5: Evaluating the potential profit and loss of an SPX put credit spread (Step 4), Source: Schwab.com

After I'm all set, I click "review order" and double-check everything. If everything looks good, I place the order, and if it is fulfilled, **$1,400 will immediately appear in my account**. Remember, it's insurance; we receive the money upfront when we sell the policy. However, it's potential profit. The cash is not mine to keep unless time passes without incident. In this case, the incident is the stock falling in price or trading below the option you sold. We make money if the stock price stays above the puts we sell. If not, we lose money. In my experience, I have more profitable trades than losers because the stock market rises over time, but your results will vary.

Finally, placing these trades may differ slightly depending on your broker, but it doesn't matter. What matters for a put credit spread is this: Always ensure you sell the higher strike put and buy the lower strike put, and ensure that you are receiving a credit into your account. Also, both options should have the same expiration date. One last thing: When you sell credit spreads, people might think, *Who will buy my credit spreads?* You're not selling to an actual person but to a "market maker" whose job is to create a market for investors to buy and sell securities.

BUYING BACK A PUT CREDIT SPREAD

You sell a credit spread to open a new position and buy it back to close the trade. Sell and then buy, the exact opposite of buy-and-hold. Again, placing these sell-and-buy orders can be confusing or intimidating initially, but it gets easier over time. I'll use the example trade profiled in Figure 4 to explain how I would close a credit spread trade. On Schwab, after placing my order, I'm taken to a confirmation screen with a button that says "review order." Once I click on that, I am taken to my order history page.

⊻	Symbol	⟨	Status ▲ ⓘ	Action ⓘ	Quantity	Order Type	Timing ⓘ	Fill Price	Bid	⟩
▶	SSPX Vertical Put Spre...		OPEN	Buy	1/1	Debit $1.40	GTC Exp 05/16/2025	-	$5.10	≡ ⌄
▶	SSPX Vertical Put Spre...		FILLED	Sell	1/1	Credit $7.60	Day	$7.60	$5.10	≡ ⌄
▶	SSPX Vertical Put Spre...		FILLED	Buy	1/1	Debit $1.50	GTC Exp 01/17/2025	$1.45	$	

Similar Order
Opposite Order

Figure 6: Creating a closing order for a credit spread, Source: Schwab.com

If I noticed the order was filled, I would click the drop-down menu and choose "opposite order," and the closing order would pull up. To open the spread, I sold the higher strike 5860 put and bought the lower strike 5850 put for an overall credit. To **close a credit spread trade**, I would reverse how I opened it. I would simultaneously "buy back" the higher strike put and then "sell" the lower strike put for an overall debit. Said another way, I would buy back the option that was initially sold and then sell the option that was initially bought. The order action this time would be "buy to close" and "sell to close" to indicate that you are closing the credit spread position. It's called buying back a spread because closing it will cost you money. You will close the pair of options for a debit.

Symbol	Strategy	Chain	S&P 500 INDEX		04:43:24 PM ET. 10/28/2024	Margin ⚑ Chart ⚑
$SPX ⌄	Vertical Put ⌄	⬀	$5823.52		Previous Close	5,808.12
			+15.4 (0.27%)		Day Range	5823.08 - 5842.92
				Today's Open	5833.93 52 Week	4103.78 - 5878.46
Action	Quantity	Chain	Option Symbol		Bid	Mid	Ask

Buy to close ⌄	— 5 +	⬀ ⬚ SPX ⌄ 04/17/2025 ⌄ 5860.00 ⌄ Put ⌄	199.40	200.3	201.20 🗑
					+ Show Full Quote
Sell to close ⌄	— 5 +	⬀ ⬚ SPX ⌄ 04/17/2025 ⌄ 5850.00 ⌄ Put ⌄	196.60	197.15	197.70 🗑
					+ Show Full Quote

+ Add a Leg   Net Quote ❶   1.70   Dr 3.15   Dr 4.60

Order type ❶	Limit price ❶	Timing ❶	Date mm/dd/yyyy	Estimated Amount:
Net debit ⌄	— 0.55 +	GTC (Good till canceled) ⌄	04/17/2025 📅	**$275.00**
				(Based on Limit Price)
				(does not include commission or fees)

Figure 7: An example of placing a GTC order to buy back five long-term SPX put credit spreads, Source: Schwab.com

A standard practice among investors who sell options is to close their positions once they have achieved roughly 80 percent of the maximum profit. So, if you sold this credit spread for a $2.80 credit, you'd multiply that figure by 0.2. Doing so would give you $0.56; I usually round down to the nearest cent and enter that number as the limit price for my closing order. When closing credit spreads, the order type should say net debit. The limit price in our example would be $0.55, and the timing would be GTC, which stands for "good till canceled." The purpose of GTC orders is to automate the closing process of profitable trades. It tells the broker to close the insurance trade for me if it is 80 percent profitable.

I set the GTC order to expire on April 17, 2025, the same day my spread expires. The GTC tells the broker to leave the closing order open until my criteria are satisfied. Once satisfied, the broker will execute the order and close the spread trade for me. If that criterion is not satisfied (I have a losing trade), the GTC will be canceled on the options expiration, and the broker will close my spread for a loss.

People often struggle with GTC orders as you give up some of your profit to close the trade early, but here is a short explanation for why we use them. It's more prudent to close trades before expiration because it's better to book 80 percent of your profit early than risk losing on the trade to earn a few extra dollars. Pretend you achieved $1,200 of your max $1,400 profit. Wouldn't it be wise to take that profit early instead of risking the chance that the market could fall? The greedy investor who holds out for that last few dollars can lose the profit and incur a $3,600 loss.

Ultimately, we have little control over whether we make money or not. It's dependent on the stock market. If the trade is a loser, the broker will close it for us at expiration and deduct the money from our account. However, if we are fortunate and the trade becomes profitable quickly, it's best to take your profit off the table.

We'll discuss profit and losses again in another chapter, but I want to encourage you to get out there and practice this yourself. Learning how to place trades via a book is like learning how to swim via a book. Nothing can replace real-world experience. You will learn more about credit spreads by selling them in real life than you can by reading about them. It took a lot of pages to go through the order process, but in real life, this takes me about five minutes from start to finish. And it takes my wife about fifteen minutes as a novice investor. That said, I want to end with a cautionary note. Selling credit spreads can be a painful learning experience for some. Therefore, in the next chapter, I want to warn you about the most dangerous method of trading credit spreads. Ironically, it's the most popular method taught in the options industry.

7

THE POPULAR BUT DANGEROUS WAY OF SELLING CREDIT SPREADS

> *I made good money on credit spreads in 2021 on TSLA and FB. When tech crashed in January 2022, I lost 85 percent of my account. I changed to selling puts to buy great companies at low prices. If the company doesn't get below my put price, I keep the premium. If it does, I buy the stock!*
>
> — COMMENT FOUND ON X (FORMERLY TWITTER)

A few disclosures before I get started: If you're new to selling credit spreads, you have no idea how controversial this chapter will be. It will upset most of the option-selling community because I will speak against the most popular way of selling credit spreads. So, if you're experienced with selling credit spreads and get offended by what I say, try not to take it personally. I'm not criticizing you as a person; I'm criticizing the math and stupidity behind the popular high-probability credit spread trade.

The chapter's quote demonstrates why I'm against the traditional way of selling credit spreads. I wish it were an uncommon experience, but it's not. So many people have destroyed their lives financially with the reckless approach taught by online gurus. Also, notice how the quote's author switched to selling put options like Warren Buffett. Do you recall what I said at the beginning of the book about modeling those who are already successful? I think we can both agree that losing 85 percent of your money with credit spreads is the opposite of success, so let me show you how to avoid that misery.

Let me first explain the popular approach: selling high-probability out-of-the-money put credit spreads. Without getting all geeky on option terminology, **out-of-the-money** (or "OTM" for short) means a credit spread with strike prices below the stock price. In theory, they are so far below the stock that there is a low probability that it will fall to that price. This means you are likely to make money. In other words, it's a credit spread where you statistically have a 70 to 90 percent chance of making money. This is precisely why so many people are attracted to this method, like flies to cow dung. However, the downfall is that you can lose significantly more than you can make.

Sadly, you don't discover this until you trade them and lose money like the gentleman above. To promote this approach, gurus use what I call mathematical wizardry. The marketing on the sales page says they rarely lose money because the strategy has a 75 percent win rate, which is a fact. However, they conveniently leave out the dollar amounts of the spread trades because it would expose this ugly truth: Even with a high win rate, you can still lose money! It's common to have eleven months of profit wiped out with one losing trade. But hey, at least you can brag about a 92 percent win rate (facepalm).

I just pulled up a high-probability spread on my broker platform. I have included the details below for you to review. I want you to look at it, using good old-fashioned common sense, and tell me if this looks like an attractive way to make money.

A High-Probability Out-of-the-Money Credit Spread Example

The S&P is trading at $6,090, and I'm looking at a 5835/5830 put credit spread (selling twenty-eight 5835 puts and buying twenty-eight 5830 puts).

- There are 56 days until expiration, and strike prices are 4% below the stock. The probability calculator on the broker platform shows that it has an 80% chance of being profitable.
- There is a $14,000 margin requirement.

- There is a potential profit of $1,540 and a possible loss of $12,460. It will equal an 11% return on the margin requirement if profitable.
- The risk/reward means it will take eight winning trades to make up for one losing trade.

If you had a $50,000 account and sold two spreads like this, more than half of your account would be tied up as a margin requirement. Also, if you're unlucky and your first two trades are losers, you're already down $24,920. Does investing your money this way seem wise to you? Would you be willing to try again after losing so much money? Even if the next trade worked out, you'd only make $1,540. Emotionally, it will feel hopeless, scary, and utterly depressing. These OTM spreads only work if you keep selling them until the probabilities work in your favor, but you won't do that if you're discouraged from losing so much money.

In all fairness, since these are high-probability spreads, you will usually go nine to eleven months without a loss. At this point, ego and greed start to kick in. *It's easy money,* you'll tell yourself, and you'll be more aggressive about making money. After all, you have a high win rate. But then, you'll have a few losing trades that will wipe you out financially. A year of hard work, all your previous profit, and most of your account value goes bye-bye! Sure, you can still proudly boast about your high win rate, but high win rates don't pay bills; money does. And you can't make money if one or two losing trades wipe you out financially. That's just common sense.

Only those with several decades of experience know I'm speaking the truth. However, when you point out this nasty reality, nearly every option guru starts to operate off a script they've been programmed with. They start talking about rolling and adjusting trades and how the probabilities will work in your favor if you keep at it. My internal dialogue is like, *Bruh! You can't roll, adjust, or keep placing spreads if you lose all your money. Once you lose all your money, it's game over; you're done. Besides, the larger margin requirement of out-of-the-money spreads locks up so much of your account that it's nearly impossible to recover from massive losses.*

Anyhoo ...

I'm not here to change the minds of experienced spread sellers. You do you. I'm more worried about the new people reading this, so let me be super blunt: Risking $12,000 to make a $1,000 profit is a stupid way to manage your money. I don't care how high the probability of profit is. Don't fall for high-win-rate marketing tricks that appeal to your egotistical desire to win on every trade. Just avoid high-probability credit spreads. By selling them, you are putting yourself in a position where you are "guaranteed" to lose a lot of money if things don't work out. Does that seem wise to you? I'm incredibly biased, but that seems dumb to me.

But I get why people do it. They don't know any better; they only know what they've been taught. They didn't realize there was a better way of selling credit spreads because 99 percent of option gurus teach the same methods. They all live in the same close-minded mental box: *This is the best way to do it. You sell spreads when the VIX is high, pick a low delta, etc. Roll the spread if you lose 50 percent of your credit or your short strike is challenged.* My response to all of that is *blah, blah, blah.*

Okay, let's put blunt Travis back in his cage and let me share a more polite perspective. Of all the rich people I've studied, <u>none</u> said they got rich by "repeatedly" engaging in transactions where they could lose significantly more money than they could make. I repeat, none! Here is what I consider a more intelligent way of managing your money. You sell credit spreads with the mindset of a patient long-term investor. Doing so, I discovered another high-probability credit spread that is much better for your emotions and bank account: long-term at-the-money spreads.

Long-term means six to twelve months out in time, and **at-the-money** (or "ATM" for short) means a credit spread with strike prices that are the same or near the stock's current price. If SPX is trading at $6,090, and I sell a 6100/6075 put credit spread, I've sold an at-the-money spread. Simply put, it's a credit spread near the stock's current price. I've never seen this taught anywhere else, and I already explained why: No one is willing to think outside the box.

Long-Term At-the-Money (ATM) Credit Spread Example

Again, the S&P is trading at $6090, but now I'm looking at a 6100/6075 put credit spread (selling two 6100 puts and buying two 6075 puts).

- There are 195 days until expiration and strike prices around the same price as the stock. The probability calculator on the broker platform shows that it has a 56% chance of being profitable, but in my experience, it's more like 75 to 80% (more on this in the next chapter).
- There is a $5,000 margin requirement, less than half of the OTM approach.
- There is a potential profit of $1,440 and a possible loss of $3,560. It will equal a 29% return on the margin requirement if profitable.
- The risk/reward means it will take two and a half winning trades to compensate for one losing trade.

With this approach, I make roughly the same profit but with less risk, a higher return on margin, and the same probability of making money. In other words, I achieve a high win rate and smaller losses. Most importantly, if I have a losing trade, my emotions are not frazzled, and that's the key to why this works better. At-the-money spreads align better with human nature. By and large, humans hate pain and will avoid it. It's why they panic sell index funds during market declines even though the wise choice is to buy more when the stock market is having a sale. Pain avoidance is also why people don't continue selling out-of-the-money spreads after a loss; they are trying to prevent more emotional suffering.

Also, with the lower margin requirement, I can place two of these for every one of the high-probability trades. This is simply a more intelligent way of managing your money, but there I go using common sense—how dare I challenge the wisdom of an online guru? Sarcasm aside, you can argue with the math all you want, but the numbers don't lie. The long-term ATM credit spread is superior in every way, but you won't discover this unless you trade them for at least six months. Finally, I gained significant insight once I switched to selling long-term spreads. Many don't have this insight because they have been programmed to believe there is only one way of trading credit spreads.

Here was my revelation: After watching the stock market rise in price for nearly thirty years, I realized that in most cases, a short-term out-of-the-money spread used to be a long-term at-the-money spread. So, instead of selling shorter-dated OTM spreads with horrible risk/rewards, I sell long-dated ATM spreads with better risk/rewards. Then, I patiently wait for them to become out-of-the-money spreads once the market rises in price. At that point, time decay takes over and rapidly melts away the value of the spread. Selling spreads this way achieves the high win rate that people are after, but when I lose, I don't give back all my profit.

A Short, Simplified Lesson on Time Decay

A little more about time decay before we move on. Part of an options premium, or cost, is time value. It's a dollar figure assigned to how many days are left until the option expires. The shorter the time to expiration, the less time value the option has. For example, options with longer expirations cost more because they provide more "time" to be right about your options hypothesis. Over time, the option's price shrinks in value due to a concept called time decay.

Time decay describes how the value of an options contract erodes or decreases as the option approaches its expiration date. In other words, a small portion of the option's value is lost each day that passes. It starts as a slow decline. Then, it speeds up the closer the option gets to its expiration date because there is less time to profit from the option contract. Picture an ice cube. You take it out of the freezer and put it in the sun. It starts melting slowly, but the longer it's in the sun, the faster it will melt.

What this looks like in practice is that if you "buy" an option, you hope it increases in value so you can sell it at a higher price before time decay eats away at it. The opposite is true when you "sell" an option. When you sell options, you love time decay and want as much of it as possible. You profit from a credit spread by selling it, and each day, without incident, its value will decrease. When most of the profit has been achieved, you repurchase it at a lower price. In other words, time decay is why we can make money with credit spreads without needing to predict the stock market's direction.

A similar process happens with car insurance policies. Imagine an agent sold me a one-year insurance policy for $1,200 (on average, $100 monthly). Each month that passes without incident, the agent gets to keep $100 of the $1,200 received upfront (time decay). However, let's pretend nine months have passed without incident, and I call to cancel my policy. Since there are still three months left in my policy, I get a refund of $300. In essence, the agent sold the policy for $1,200 and repurchased it for $300, thus making a profit of $900. That's an analogy of buying a credit spread back for less than you sold it for.

ANOTHER REASON I DON'T SELL HIGH-PROBABILITY SPREADS

Math and common sense seemed to be the primary reasons I don't sell high-probability credit spreads, but they're only part of the reason. Another reason is that I invested based on probabilities nearly two decades ago and went bankrupt. However, it was with real estate, not credit spreads. It emotionally scarred me, so now I'm conservative with my money. I'm super sensitive about losing large sums of money. Let me quickly share that cautionary tale so you can see another example of the danger of investing based on high probabilities.

After years of buying properties, I became a real estate millionaire and quit my job. However, I let my success get to my head, got greedy, and overleveraged myself. I invested 100 percent of my money because I wanted to be wealthier. I kept no money in savings. My mentor told me to keep six months of mortgage payments in savings for each property, but I was hard-headed and didn't listen. Things were going great, so I invested based on that reality; I didn't plan for anything to go wrong. Well, something did go wrong—horribly wrong!

I had about seven to ten separate units spread across town, and every tenant decided to move out the same month. All my properties went vacant at the same time! What's the probability of that happening? Low, right? Well, it did happen, and not only did I have thousands of dollars in mortgage payments, but most of the units needed repairs. Remember, I had no savings! I paid my expenses via credit cards for as long as possible but eventually went bankrupt.

I gave up on the dream of becoming a millionaire and returned to corporate America. This is when I met my wife, at my lowest point. She saw what was in my heart and believed in me when I didn't believe in myself. With her encouragement and my knowledge of "how" to build wealth, I pulled myself out of a two-year depression and decided to pursue options trading. This time, I succeeded. It also helped that we paid off all remaining debt, lived on one income, and invested the other income.

Looking back, I realize that going broke taught me several valuable lessons, which I now apply to options trading. One of those is that probabilities are just that—probabilities. They are not guarantees. Investing based on the probability that everything will go right is a greed-focused approach. The more prudent approach is to consider everything going wrong and structure your finances to survive the worst-case scenario.

In other words, I started focusing on how to get rich without going broke in the process. Well, selling high-probability credit spreads or overleveraging with real estate are not ways of accomplishing that. **You win at investing by managing risk, not by chasing probabilities.** The profits will take care of themselves if you diligently manage the risk of loss and avoid massively stupid money mistakes. My mentor was living proof of that; he got rich by being risk-averse. That's what he was trying to teach me when he told me to keep over $100K in savings to prepare for vacancies.

My mentor viewed $100K in savings as protection (prudence). My poor, greedy mindset viewed it as a downpayment on three more properties (greed). That leads to another lesson I learned: <u>strategies and tools are not the key to success</u>. You also need the proper mindset to go along with it. So, sadly, credit spreads won't make your life better if your mindset is screwed up.

In my instance, I was being mentored by a real estate millionaire. He told me exactly what to do (strategies). I should have gotten rich, but instead, I went broke. I was using the tools of a rich person, but I had the mindset of an impatient and greedy poor person. So, sure, you're learning how to use the tools of the wealthy (credit spreads), but you also need the mindset of a rich person if you want to succeed with them. That's why, in the next chapter, I'll show you how to use spreads while modeling the mindset of a successful long-term buy-and-hold investor like Buffett.

8

THE UNCONVENTIONAL BUT MORE PROFITABLE WAY OF SELLING SPREADS

> *The stock market is a device for transferring money from the impatient to the patient.*

— WARREN BUFFETT

In the last chapter, I badmouthed the most popular form of selling credit spreads. Therefore, I think it's only fair that I spend additional time explaining why long-term at-the-money credit spreads are better. I discovered this by being curious and willing to challenge the status quo. I started questioning every belief about investing and experimented with proven concepts from other industries. More particularly, I studied successful buy-and-hold investors and applied their principles to credit spread trading. The results blew me away.

- My win rate on investments increased.
- I have more free time.
- I make more money.
- I have less stress.

And most importantly, my portfolio won't blow up from a series of losing trades. Most people sell high-probability credit spreads and ignore the massive risk of loss. They assume they will be around to manage the trade. However, if your portfolio's performance depends on you showing up to manage it, <u>you are in a dangerous situation if you have a stroke, become incapacitated, or pass away</u>. Many plan for the risk of the stock market falling, but few plan for life risk.

OTM VERSUS ATM CREDIT SPREADS

Experienced credit spread traders love out-of-the-money spreads, but there's nothing special about them. They profit from the same thing at-the-money spreads do: time decay. It's just that out-of-the-money spreads have a "theoretical" probability of being more profitable, but in my experience, managing risk and reward is more important than the probability of profit. Risk/reward is the balance between how much money you can make and how much you can lose. I sell at-the-money credit spreads because they have a better risk/reward than out-of-the-money spreads.

However, most investors don't sell at-the-money spreads because they assume they'll have low win rates. Reviewing an at-the-money credit spread on your broker platform will show that it has about a 50 percent chance of being profitable. So, most investors choose the out-of-the-money credit spread because the broker states it has a 75 to 80 percent chance of being profitable. However, out-of-the-money spreads have a horrible risk/reward where you can lose significantly more money than you can potentially make.

By choosing the at-the-money spread, I accept a "theoretical" lower probability of profit for a better risk/reward. Remember, though, probabilities are not guarantees, and in my experience, the broker's probabilities are wrong! People are so busy listening to gurus preach about manufactured probabilities that they never step back and observe how the stock market behaves in real life. So, let me share what I have observed after watching the stock market for nearly three decades. It shouldn't be a surprise because you've probably heard it before.

Historically, the stock market goes up more often than it goes down. I have noticed that the S&P 500 has more winning months than losing months in rising markets. If you go back ten years and count all the winning and losing months, I'm sure the results will be around a 70 percent win rate. So, selling at-the-money spreads gives me the high win rate that people are after, but I don't give back all my profit when I lose. I ignore the broker's probability figures and never look at them. I align myself with the only probability that matters: the long-term history of the stock market. The stock market goes up more than it goes down. Thus, I invest based on this historical fact. Now, let's discuss why I show up once a month to sell an at-the-money credit spread.

DOLLAR COST AVERAGE CREDIT SPREADS

Dollar-cost averaging (DCA) is regularly investing a fixed dollar amount, regardless of the stock's price. You may already do this if you have an employer retirement account. Usually, a set amount comes out of your monthly paycheck, and it's invested into the stock market. The opposite of dollar-cost averaging is market timing, which is trying to pinpoint the perfect time to enter and exit the market. It's hard to do, even for professional investors, so dollar-cost averaging ensures you get the "average" performance of the stock market.

So that's essentially what I do with my credit spread trades. I dollar-cost average into the market each month with a six- to twelve-month at-the-money credit spread. Since we've already established that the market's long-term performance is positive, my credit spread results are also positive, not negative. And this "includes" all the losing spreads I'll have along the way. However, in my experience, I rarely lose money with DCA spreads, and the next section explains why.

THE SECRET TO LONG-TERM ATM SPREADS

Before we begin, let me take a moment to address a common question: "Okay, Travis, I get the concept of dollar-cost averaging, but why don't you do that with thirty to sixty-day OTM or even ATM spreads? Shouldn't it work the same?" Let me address the OTM part first. Yes, DCA out-of-the-money spreads could work, but it still doesn't solve the main issue; their risk/reward sucks. As an investor, your most important job is managing the risk of loss, and anyone who understands that would not fall in love with out-of-the-money spreads.

Now, would the DCA approach work for short-term at-the-money spreads? Yes, it does. However, following that approach, I only make money on about 70 percent of trades. That makes sense, considering the historical performance discussed earlier. I eventually switched to long-term spreads because I stumbled across data that helped me increase my win rate. Translation: It helps me make more money, and that is the goal, after all.

The piece of data: The probability of a positive return in the S&P 500 increases as the holding period lengthens. If you own shares of the S&P for one year, your probability of profit is 69 percent. If you own shares for ten years, your probability of profit increases to 88 percent (Jennewine 2024). This is one of the reasons Warren Buffett is so rich; he buys companies and then holds onto them for a long time. After discovering this statistic, I wanted to know if extending the time frame would improve the success rate of my option trades. Spoiler alert: It does.

Instead of buying options that expired in three months, I started buying options that expired in three years. Instead of selling credit spreads that expired in six weeks, I started selling credit spreads that expired in six months. In both cases, buying longer-term call options and selling longer-term spreads, I made more money—way more! Does this approach take more discipline and patience? Sure, but those are two necessary ingredients for success, and the more I develop those qualities, the better investor I become. Patience = Profits.

With long-term spreads, I'm giving the stock market plenty of time to rise. By the time my spreads are ready to expire, the market is far from the strike price of the puts, and time decay is rapidly accelerating. Once the spread reaches its profit target, the GTC order closes the trade for me. Some additional benefits of long-term spreads are that my win rate increased to 80 to 90 percent and my stress level went down. Time spent managing my investments was also reduced to ten minutes a month versus several hours a week. Let me explain why my win rate is so high:

1. I only sell credit spreads in bull markets.
2. Dollar-cost averaging allows me to get the overall positive return of the market.

3. Long-term spreads allow me to sidestep their biggest threat, market corrections.

Market declines are the biggest threat to short-term spreads. I avoid that danger altogether by going out six to twelve months in time. Less losing trades mean a higher win rate. Remember, credit spreads are an insurance trade. **They don't need the stock market to move to make money.** They profit from the passing of time without incident. In our case, the most significant incident to concern ourselves with is the S&P declining in price 5 to 15 percent, which happens on average once a year. These are called market corrections.

Market corrections are usually short-lived, and eventually, the stock market recovers and goes back up. In my experience, the entire process is about six months from the start of the fall to its full recovery. Sometimes, the recovery is quick and sometimes long, but on average, it's about six months. I encourage you to review previous market corrections and see how long the recovery took on average (trust, but verify). You'll also be able to visually see how I achieve an 80 to 90 percent win rate on long-term spreads.

If I sell a long-term credit spread at the market top and it has a correction, I have plenty of time to wait out the price recovery. Of course, I can expect to lose on all my open trades during a bear market, but as you'll discover in the next chapter, I ensure that the loss is a max of 10 percent of my account. I can recover from that loss more quickly than trying to make up for an 85 percent decline in my account because I sold an out-of-the-money credit spread.

Before we end, let's discuss the investment returns from spreads. Credit spreads are defined risk strategies, so the amount I can make and lose on a long-term at-the-money spread is predictable. It's one of the reasons I don't have a ten- to fifteen-year case study in this book; there is no need. As suggested earlier, it's easy to see how much one could have made each year by reviewing past stock price history. However, please keep in mind that you can't pay bills with spreadsheet data from the past. You can only pay bills with real money you've earned. That means you have to shake off the comfort of the sidelines and get out there and do this.

That said, let me share a fictitious example. Imagine I have a $100,000 account and sell the at-the-money credit spread shared in the previous chapter. It had a potential profit of $1,440 and a possible loss of $3,560. If I win 80 to 90 percent of these types of trades, can you see how I can achieve those outrageous monthly income examples shared earlier in the book? However, can I guarantee you'll have a high win rate or profit like I do? No, but I will share my template in the next chapter and provide a proof-of-concept exercise for you to follow. I encourage you to try it out and see what type of results you get.

DCA Credit Spreads (Bonus Method)

In addition to at-the-money spreads, I occasionally sell long-term, 1 to 2 percent in-the-money (ITM) credit spreads. In-the-money means selling puts at a strike price higher than the stock price. They used to give me a 1:1 risk/reward. This means that what I could make was often the same as what I could lose. That helped me manage my risk of loss better. The trade-off is that it lowers your win rate because the stock has to move higher for you to hit your maximum profit. However, I rarely use this approach anymore. When the government raised interest rates, it screwed up this approach. Those same ITM spreads no longer have a 1:1 risk/reward.

In summary, the secret to my high win rate and credit spread returns is this: I use the tools of a trader with the mindset of a long-term buy-and-hold investor. There's no daily stock chart reviewing. I don't watch CNBC, use Option Greeks, or expensive software. And I definitely don't have an obsession with the volatility index (the VIX); I never look at it. I calculate a few numbers and follow the proven principles of a buy-and-hold investor. It's counter-intuitive and unconventional, but it works.

However, if you tell an experienced spread trader about dollar-cost averaging with long-term at-the-money credit spreads, they may reject that approach. They may also tell you why it won't work and how you only have a 50 percent chance of making money. Then, they will say that selling high-probability, out-of-the-money spreads is better. Like parrots, they repeat what they've heard a million times elsewhere. Please note: They speak from a theoretical standpoint, but I speak from experience.

I "know" selling at-the-money credit spreads work because I've been quietly following this approach behind the scenes for years. I've made more money with the at-the-money approach than the out-of-the-money approach. I have yet to find an OTM spread approach with a higher return on risk than the one I achieve, and I doubt I ever will. It's hard to grow your account when a few losing trades can wipe you out. The internet is flooded with stories of people who lost most of their money with high-probability credit spreads.

The ones who succeed with spreads don't focus on theoretical manufactured probabilities but prudently manage the risk of loss. And the long-term, dollar-cost average, at-the-money credit spread helps you do that. It's been my secret to consistent income without the pain of massive losses. I want it to be your reality as well. So, I encourage you to implement the approach taught in this book. When you do, you'll discover the same thing I did. Long-term at-the-money DCA spreads are more profitable and less stressful than short-term, out-of-the-money spreads.

9

A PROVEN CASH FLOW TEMPLATE

> *Complexity makes you look smart. Simplicity makes you money.*
>
> — CODIE SANCHEZ

While serving in the US Army, I met a millionaire who shared his blueprint for financial freedom. He introduced this working-class kid to a reality I didn't even know existed—a world where your money works for you versus you working for it. For a moment, I want you to imagine your job is to manage a business. As a manager, you don't perform the everyday physical tasks. Instead, you visit the office monthly to direct others to do the work. You'd...

- Check on the employees and assign tasks for the next few months

- Oversee the usual maintenance and upkeep of the business
- Review the overall profit or loss for the month

You only <u>spend about ten minutes in the office</u>. Afterward, you are free to do what you please with your life until next month, when you'll show up to repeat the above process. Best of all, the business consistently pays you enough money to live the life of your dreams. Imagine having a job like that. Would you want to quit a job that takes minimal time but pays well? Or could you see yourself managing that business for a long time? If so, I have good news for you.

You don't have to imagine it because that dream job can be yours! I just described the life thousands of investors worldwide live. That "business" is the stock market, and your "employees" are the dollars you have invested in the stock market. If you apply the techniques taught in this book, I'm confident the ten-minute investor lifestyle can become your reality one day. The same reality my millionaire mentor revealed to me.

Better yet, in this chapter, I'll show you how to achieve the ten-minute investor lifestyle. **The simple steps below are how I take ten minutes of free time and turn it into consistent cash flow.** I know that sounds like hype, but it's a fact. I recorded my wife and kids following this simple process to see how long a beginner would take to do this once they were given instructions. Before the steps are revealed, here are a few important disclaimers.

I'm not a certified financial planner and can't tell you what trades to make or give you any trade recommendations. I am sharing what works for me for educational purposes only. I will show you how I invest my money, but if you follow this process, you do so at your own risk. You are solely responsible for your investment results. Your results may differ from mine. I hope they are better, but there is a possibility they could be worse.

All investing has risk, and anyone who tells you they never lose money is lying. I'm a former US investing champion, and I even lose money from time to time. Sometimes, a little, sometimes a lot, but overall, my investment accounts increase over time. Finally, there are probably hundreds of ways to sell credit spreads, but this is the approach I follow because it satisfies the criteria I use to evaluate investment strategies:

- Is this passive and profitable?
- Can it be implemented in ten minutes or less?
- If I pass away or become incapacitated, can my portfolio survive that risk?

The blueprint below answers those questions with a yes, so let me show you my passive ten-minute cash flow template.

MY FOUR-STEP PASSIVE INCOME BLUEPRINT

This trading plan is what I taught to my wife and kids. This may not suit everyone's style or preference, but it gives you a starting point for your passive income journey. However, **before you invest real money, practice on paper first!** Paper or virtual trading is a process where you pretend to invest your money and keep a record of your transactions. Do that until you have a track record of successful pretend trades. Check with your broker to see if they have a paper trading platform. Or, like me, you can use old-fashioned pen and paper.

By following this prudent paper trading approach, you will be modeling the success of the airline and medical industry. After all, do they let new pilots fly airplanes with real people in them, or do they let medical students practice on real humans first? No, they don't. In summary, trading with real money when you don't know what you are doing is unwise. There's a lot of dumb money floating around in the stock market, but don't let it be yours. Never risk real money until you have a solid understanding and a good track record of profit on paper.

That said, here is the <u>monthly</u> four-step process I use to place my credit spread trades. I tend to sell my credit spreads in the last week of the month, while others place theirs at the beginning. The key is to have a routine and stay consistent. Regardless, each step is designed to reduce the risk of experiencing a massive loss. And when you do that, making money becomes more effortless.

Step 1: Is It Hurricane Season?

Do you like losing money? I don't, so I do not sell put credit spreads during bear or downward-trending markets (hurricane season). When stocks fall, people exercise their put insurance, and that's when you will lose money on the put credit spreads you sell. I only sell stock insurance when investors are least likely to use it. This means I only sell put credit spreads during bull or upward-rising markets.

Here's an analogy to help you understand the purpose of this question. If you sell a six-month homeowners insurance policy during hurricane season, there's a high likelihood you'll have to pay out a claim (i.e., lose money). However, if you wait until hurricane season ends to sell insurance, you increase your chances of making money.

The following are two simple ways of determining whether it's hurricane season in the stock market. First is the simplified approach for beginner investors who don't understand moving averages. Remember, this is an insurance trade, so you want to ensure you are not placing a trade in the middle of a bear market.

- Find a website where you can pull up a one-year stock chart of the S&P 500.

- Make sure the stock chart has an overall upward trend for the last year. If it's been trending up the last year, it's reasonably safe to place this trade. However, if the right side of the stock chart is lower than the left side, the market is falling, and you should not open a put credit spread.

If you are a more advanced investor and know how to add a moving average to a stock chart, here's another approach. To determine whether we are in a bull or bear market, ask the following risk-based question: **Is the S&P 500 above or below the 200-day simple moving average (200-DMA)?** The answer is not based on how many days above or below; it's a simple yes or no answer. If above the 200-DMA, I sell put credit spreads on SPX. If below, I do not place a trade. I sit on my hands and patiently wait for the S&P to return above the 200-day simple moving average.

If the S&P 500 is above the 200-day simple moving average, we are in a bull market, and prices are rising on average (i.e., it's not hurricane season). This means that every bullish credit spread I place is more likely to be profitable. If the S&P 500 is below the 200-day simple moving average, that's the equivalent of hurricane season. Yeah, no thanks, I won't sell insurance; it's too dangerous. Could I make money anyway? Possibly, but why take the extra risk when I don't have to?

Also, could I reverse the template and sell bearish credit spreads, which profit during down markets? I could, but bear markets are too volatile, and I don't like the extra work. I instead choose to subdue my greed, take a break from selling spreads, and live off savings or dividend income during bear markets. It gives me a chance to practice discipline and patience. However, don't let my bias stop you from earning income in bear markets. If you use both bullish and bearish spreads, you will generate consistent monthly income in any market environment.

Finally, this is not a step I perform each month—I only have to do it once or twice a year. If the stock market goes up after I've looked at it, I know there is no need to perform this step again. However, if the stock market has fallen 10 to 20 percent, I'll peek at the stock chart to see if Step 1 is still satisfied.

Step 2: How Much Money Do I Want to Lose?

This is yet another risk-related step, and I want you to notice how the question is asked. It's not focused on making money! Prudent investors focus on the risk of loss first and profits second. Greedy investors focus too much on making money, don't adequately plan for losses, and then wonder why they can't grow their accounts. Getting rich in the stock market is counterintuitive. Most people think you need to find an outstanding stock or strategy that will deliver high returns, but I haven't seen that to be the case. I achieved financial freedom by eliminating the most significant threat to my success, and that's experiencing huge investment losses.

With each of these steps, I try to minimize or lower the chance of experiencing an account-crippling loss. So, with Step 2, I control how much money I lose if things don't work out as planned. Please note: I didn't say I'm trying to avoid a loss. I expect to have losses, but the best way to avoid losing a lot of money is to never put yourself in a position to lose a lot. That's why I follow the 2/10 formula.

I will risk roughly 2 percent of my account per credit spread trade. That means the potential loss on each spread will be approximately 2 percent of my account value. Also, with this strategy, I will have a maximum of 10 percent of my account value at risk at any given time. This 10 percent cap means that if we enter a bear market, the most I could lose on this one strategy is 10 percent of my account. Please note: When I say "account," I mean all the money we have invested in the stock market, even if it's spread among several accounts. That said, here's a simple way to follow the 2/10 formula:

- Place a credit spread, and ensure that the maximum loss on the spread is roughly 2% of your account value.

- Have no more than five of these low-risk credit
  spread trades open at any given time.

Here's an example of what this might look like if I had $40,000 in an employer retirement plan and $20,000 in an individual retirement account (IRA). Since you can't trade options in most company retirement plans, the spreads must go inside the IRA. The 2/10 calculation would be based on $60,000. First, I multiply the $60K account size by .02, which gives me $1,200.

So, for every credit spread I open, I want to ensure the maximum I can lose is roughly $1,200. It will never be exact, but I want to be close to this figure. In practice, the max loss on a trade might be $2,400, but I would look to close the trade once I lost roughly $1,200 (2 percent of my account value). I'd continue selling spreads like this until my total potential losses on all open trades equal $12,000 (10 percent of my account). Once I reach my limit, I stop placing new trades until one closes.

Calculating the 2/10 values is also a step I do not perform monthly. I calculate my values at the beginning of the year during my portfolio's annual rebalance and use those numbers all year. My account value does not fluctuate much during a year, so doing this calculation once a year saves me time. Finally, using this formula means I no longer get stressed when the market falls. I take my tiny loss and move on with my life. I can compensate for the loss with another spread or buy-and-hold stock shares.

Step 3: Do I Want to Be Patient or Impatient?

In the first step, I determined whether it's a safe environment to sell put credit spreads. If it were, then most likely, I'd make money. However, since the future is unpredictable, I planned for the worst by calculating how much money I would lose if the trade didn't work out. In Step 3, I sell the credit spread and pick one of three approaches. All three work, and what you choose comes down to personal preference and your level of patience.

1. **Selling short-term spreads with expirations one to five months in the future.** You'll book profits quicker but will have more losing trades due to market corrections.

2. **Selling long-term spreads with expirations six to twelve months in the future (my preferred choice).** You'll have a higher win rate because you have enough time to survive market corrections. However, you'll need to be more patient because booking your profit will take several months.

3. **Selling both short- and long-term spreads, a hybrid approach.** This is a compromise between the two above methods. If you take this approach, you usually split your 2 percent risk and place two monthly trades (1 percent risk each).

I only want to "work" once a month, so as long as Step 1 is satisfied, I show up at the end of the month, pick one of these choices, and sell an at-the-money credit spread. Again, at-the-money is a term that describes the option with a strike price that is closest to or at the same price as the stock. I usually stick with the broker's default strike prices of the spread and ensure I have enough cash in my account to handle the margin requirement of the spread I am selling. Also, since I'm using SPX, it always has enough trading volume for my order to go through smoothly.

Step 4: I Hire an Employee to Manage My Business

I submit a GTC order to close my credit spread once it has achieved roughly 80 percent of its maximum profit (credit received × 0.2 = GTC buyback price). The GTC order is like an employee who manages my insurance business so I don't have to. The only time I need to invest in this process is the few minutes it takes to sell the spread. After that, I outsource the management of the spread to someone else. Closing the spread early for a profit also frees up the money used for the margin requirement. Once the cash is free, I can use it for another spread I want to sell. Another reason I automate the closing of profitable trades is because it takes the risk of loss off the table. It prevents a profitable trade from turning into a losing trade.

However, if this 80 percent profit target is not achieved, the broker will close the spread for me on its expiration day. Either way, this is a set-it-and-forget-it process for me. I show up once a month, click a few buttons, and watch cash flow into my account. Then, I sit back and let the stock market do all the work of earning passive income for me. If the stock market does what it has historically done, it will rise higher over time, and I'll make money on the spread trade. In the rare case where I lose money, I'll incur a small but manageable loss of 2 percent of my investment account.

In summary, since I only sell SPX spreads with no risk of stock assignment, I don't manage them. The GTC order either repurchases them at 80 percent profit, or I accept a max loss at expiration, which the broker handles for me.

————

Some investors will distrust the once-a-month dollar-cost average approach. They will tell themselves, *It's too simple; there's no way it can be that profitable.* They are convinced that complicated equals more profitable. It's a weird quirk of human nature. We discount simple but effective things and are attracted to complex but less effective ones. Ultimately, you don't win any awards for making investing more complicated; you only make your life harder.

So, if you want to complicate this process, I want you to stop and ask yourself this: I was taught a simple system that allows Travis to achieve above-average market returns, and it only takes ten minutes a month to implement. Why is that not good enough for me? Why am I tweaking it and adding unnecessary complexity? Most importantly, do my tweaks improve performance?

> *Complexity is your enemy. Any fool can make something complicated. It is hard to keep things simple.*
>
> — SIR RICHARD BRANSON

Finally, I want to end by circling back to the lifestyle mentioned at the start of the chapter—a world where you show up once a month to manage a business. You don't perform the physical labor of working all month; the stock market and your employees (i.e., your money) do that for you. Your only job is to assign tasks and tell employees what to do. It's the ten-minute investor lifestyle, and you have just discovered how to achieve it. However, please don't believe it naively. I want you to be intellectually curious: "Trust, but verify." I'll show you exactly how to do that in the next chapter.

10

SHOWING YOU THE MONEY

This week marks the end of my fourth month following your plan. And with today's big move up, I'm now into six figures—no, not the account—the earnings! Dang, you scammer. LOL. This is nucking futs. I mean, it's so flippin' easy. I'm just sitting around bored because there is nothing to do ... and I'm making more than before .... way more. So thank you very much for what you have taught and for having one of the "cheapest" systems out there.

— CHARLES

When Charles sent me the above email, it was the first time I'd enjoyed being called a scammer. I also want you to have results like his or better, and this chapter is written with that goal in mind. In full disclosure, I didn't verify his results, but since most of humanity is honest, I believe he is telling the truth. As an author and wealth-building coach, I appreciate people like Charles. He did what unsuccessful people are unwilling to do: He took action!

Compare that to the many skeptical people who email me. They, too, call me a scammer and then angrily demand that I show them my brokerage statements and tax returns. Like an idiot, I used to jump through hoops and fulfill requests like that. Do you think I won them over? Nope! I then got accused of sending fake photo-shopped brokerage statements (facepalm).

The request would then shift to this: "I don't believe these statements are real. Teach me for free, and then I'll pay you." I'm hard-headed and a slow learner, but I eventually discovered the secret to overcoming skepticism: **Inspire people to _act_ on what I teach.** Don't show them my trades, prior results, or fifteen-year case studies. Instead, get them to implement the strategy, and then they will have all the proof they need to determine whether this is the real deal (or not). With that realization in mind, I have a message for you.

The safest approach is to paper trade the concepts taught in this book. If it works for you, great. If not, I hope you find another system that helps you achieve your goals. Said more bluntly: Freaking implement what you learn!

Accumulating more information is often a sophisticated form of procrastination. Prioritize doing!

The passive income blueprint shared in the previous chapter has helped my family earn thousands of dollars in passive income every month. However, only those who implement, like Charles, discover this secret. So stop sitting on the sidelines, living in fear. Implement, implement, implement. After all, what would feel better: sending you a broker statement showing you my money or **six figures of profit sitting in your account?**

If you want to be the person with real-world results, let me share the secret to achieving those results. You have to implement what I teach just like Charles did. I'm even going to help you. I will guide you through a low-risk way to verify that the cash flow strategy works and can help you generate passive income.

YOUR PROOF-OF-CONCEPT EXERCISE

There are two ways I can show you the money. I can show you broker statements, which reveal how much money I make. But all that does is show you "my" money, sitting in "my" account and making "my" life better. You will be no better off after receiving the proof. The other way of showing you the money is helping you achieve similar investment returns as the ones shared earlier in the book. Of course, I can't guarantee you will succeed. I can only teach you how I do it. Since I know some people won't paper trade as I suggested, I want to share a low-risk real-money approach to consider. Just understand that if you follow this process, you do so at your own risk. You are solely responsible for your investment results.

We Start with a Prudent Mindset

First, you start with the proper mindset because success with money is 80 percent mental and 20 percent strategy. Strategies like credit spreads are just tools, and you will never succeed with the tool unless you have the mindset of a prudent investor. Therefore, I'm walking you through how I would approach this if I were an entrepreneur starting a new insurance business. In this business, I will sell stock insurance to wealthy investors. I also know that I can't control the stock market or predict what it will do. This means I can't predict if the business will make money.

However, I can control how much I am willing to lose with this new business venture, so that will be my priority. In other words, my priority is not making money. People who fail focus on making money. Instead, I will set up a system so the money comes to me. But if things don't work out, I won't go bankrupt. With that in mind, no matter how large my account is, I am setting aside $5,000 that I'm willing to lose.

With this stock insurance business, my startup cost is the margin requirement for the credit spreads I sell. When I sell credit spreads, the broker holds some of my cash to cover the risk of a loss if the stock falls in price. If the stock rises and the spread is closed early for a profit, the broker will release the cash held as a margin requirement. So, the $5,000 will be distributed among several credit spread trades. Finally, I will devote more money to the process if I'm fortunate and the business profits.

Placing the Trade

Now, let's talk about the system you'll use so that money comes to you without you physically working for it. It's the same four steps you learned in the previous chapter.

Step 1: Is It Safe Enough to Sell a Spread?

Only sell put credit spreads in an upward-rising market. If that's the case when you read this, it's safe to sell a put credit spread.

Step 2: The 2/10 Formula

You can skip this step for now. We addressed our risk by capping our loss at $5,000. However, if you decide to integrate this strategy into your overall investment plan, you will use the 2/10 formula.

Step 3: Short-Term or Long-Term?

If you're a novice spread seller, you don't know the pros and cons of selling short-term versus long-term spreads, so do both. Implement the hybrid approach and learn in real time. Pick a time during the month to sell a credit spread (beginning, middle, or end), and stick with it for the duration of the exercise. In Month 1 of doing this, place two trades: Sell an at-the-money put credit spread that expires in roughly two months (sixty days) and a credit spread that expires in approximately six months (180 days). **For both spreads, sell one contract only!**

Then, in Months 2 and 3, repeat this process of showing up once a month and selling a sixty-day and 180-day at-the-money put credit spread. Sell one contract only and stick to the default strike prices the broker gives you for those time frames. Just ensure you sell a higher strike put option, buy a lower strike put option, and **receive a credit into your account.**

I've performed this process myself in preparing for this book, and after the above three months, I still have some of my $5,000 left over that the broker didn't hold as margin. This amount is used for two more trades. In Months 4 and 5, sell one long-dated at-the-money spread and add it after the farthest-dated spread you have open. For example, if the longest-dated spread you have open is October, open a November credit spread. If you followed the above process, these last two spreads should have roughly six to seven months until expiration. Here is a quick recap:

- **Month 1:** Sell one 60-days till expiration (DTE) spread and one 180-DTE spread. It won't be exact; get close enough to two and six months until expiration.

- **Month 2:** Sell one 60-DTE and one 180-DTE spread (leave your previous two spreads in place).
- **Month 3:** Sell one 60-DTE and one 180-DTE spread (leave any previous spreads in place).
- **Month 4:** Sell one long-term spread 180-200 DTE (leave any previous spreads in place).
- **Month 5:** Sell one long-term spread 180-200 DTE (ensure it expires after the month 4 spread).

Again, I did this myself, and here is a summary of what it looked like:

- In September 2024, I sold an SPX November 2024 5730/5725 credit spread for $170 (the 60-day spread) and an SPX March 2025 5730/5720 spread for $295 (the 180-day spread).
- In October 2024, I sold an SPX December 2024 5805/5800 credit spread for $165 (the 60-day spread) and an SPX April 2025 5810/5800 spread for $300 (the 180-day spread).
- From here, I'd rinse and repeat until all five months are complete.

Again, I sell one contract for each spread and stick with the broker's default strike prices for the spreads I want to sell. Once you have experience, you can play around with the strike prices of the put. For now, just get used to the process of selling credit spreads.

Step 4: Place a GTC Order

Automate the closing of profitable trades with GTC orders. Please put in a GTC order to repurchase the spread when it has achieved 80 percent of its profit. That calculation was shown in a previous chapter. Also, since we are using SPX, which is cash-settled, you can let the broker close losing trades for you. Remember, you're managing a business, not working in it. Please note: If this were a spread on a stock, there would be a risk of stock assignment, so it would have to be managed constantly and potentially closed manually!

Managing the Credit Spread

I sell these spreads monthly, and they are zero-management trades. After I sell the spread, I don't touch it ever again. Either I will make money, or I won't. There's no risk of stock assignment, and I've already factored in an acceptable loss. Remember, I'm dollar-cost averaging into the market, and with that process, I accept that not every spread will be a winner. If the stock rises and it's a winning trade, my good-till-canceled order will close it. If the stock falls in price and it's a losing trade, the broker will close the spread for me and deduct the loss from my account balance.

I only need to show up for the five minutes it takes me to place a trade, and then I'm done with it forever. I let the broker and the stock market take over from there. In my experience, the less I'm involved with this process, the more money I make (your results may vary). Besides, working more defeats the whole purpose of earning passive income. Never forget that point.

Another important reminder is that selling a credit spread generates instant cash flow. However, don't confuse cash flow with profit. The credit or money received when you sell the credit spread is a "potential" profit. We produce cash flow each month from selling stock insurance policies, and the profit-taking, if there is any, happens once the policy has ended. We end the policy by buying back profitable spreads early or letting them expire for a loss.

How to Watch Me Do This for Free

You are now faced with a choice. I shared the ten-minute template that allows me to beat the market and generate consistent income. You were even provided a proof-of-concept exercise so you can validate every claim made in this book. However, will this be another book you read but don't apply the information? Will you become a knowledge zombie that aimlessly wanders around collecting more information but never "doing" anything with the information? Or will you take action and join thousands of other investors living in passive income paradise?

The people who ultimately succeed with the credit spread strategy have mastered the speed of implementation (i.e., how quickly you go from a new concept to execution). Those who take quick action on new ideas succeed, while those who don't fail. If you're an action-taker like Charles and are ready to "trust but verify," don't let me stop you. Get after it.

With just $5,000 and five months of commitment, you'll have all the proof you need of this strategy's effectiveness. Based on your results, you can decide whether to integrate this strategy into your overall investment plan. Best of all, this entire four-step process takes, on average, ten minutes. For some people, however, it might take a bit longer. Regardless, it's still less time than you would spend at an office working for someone else.

One more thing before we move on: Seeing these instructions written versus doing them in real life is an entirely different experience. As an author, I want to do my best to support you, so I recorded a free video tutorial to walk you through this simple ten-minute process. **No email opt-in is required, and you won't be added to my newsletter or offered products to buy.** You can watch the short video and then return to reading this book.

I'll even share the results I achieved from following this same proof-of-concept exercise. To watch the video, visit www.tradertravis.com/tutorial.html.

11

QUESTIONS ABOUT MANAGING CREDIT SPREADS

> *Only a fool learns from his own mistakes. The wise man learns from the mistakes of others.*
>
> — OTTO VON BISMARCK

People who have mastered selling credit spreads love them and the passive income they generate. However, the math of the spread and how complicated it looks in your account can be frustrating and confusing. One question I frequently receive is, "How can I tell if I made money on the spread?" I'll answer this using the example trades I placed for the proof-of-concept (POC) exercise.

On September 25, 2024, I sold a short-term at-the-money spread with a November 2024 expiration and a long-term ATM spread with a March 2025 expiration. Then, on

October 23, 2024, I repeated this process of selling one short-term and one long-term credit spread. This is the suggested hybrid approach for the POC exercise. To simplify this process, I placed a GTC order to close all these trades at $0.40. Figure 8 shows the transaction history from my brokerage account.

Date	Action	Symbol	Quantity	Price	Fees & Comm	Amount
9/25/2024	Buy to Open	SPX 11/15/2024 5725.00 P	1	$103.69	$1.29	($10,370.29)
9/25/2024	Sell to Open	SPX 11/15/2024 5730.00 P	1	$105.39	$1.29	$10,537.71
11/6/2024	Sell to Close	SPX 11/15/2024 5725.00 P	1	$10.50	$1.29	$1,048.71
11/6/2024	Buy to Close	SPX 11/15/2024 5730.00 P	1	$10.90	$1.29	($1,091.29)
9/25/2024	Buy to Open	SPX 03/21/2025 5720.00 P	1	$182.17	$1.29	($18,218.29)
9/25/2024	Sell to Open	SPX 03/21/2025 5730.00 P	1	$185.12	$1.29	$18,510.71
10/23/2024	Buy to Open	SPX 12/20/2024 5800.00 P	1	$121.87	$1.29	($12,188.29)
10/23/2024	Sell to Open	SPX 12/20/2024 5805.00 P	1	$123.52	$1.29	$12,350.71
10/23/2024	Sell to Open	SPX 04/17/2025 5810.00 P	1	$196.85	$1.29	$19,683.71
10/23/2024	Buy to Open	SPX 04/17/2025 5800.00 P	1	$193.85	$1.29	($19,386.29)

Figure 8: Credit spreads I sold for the proof-of-concept exercise, Source: Schwab.com

Please don't be intimated by all the numbers. I'll explain everything and will summarize what you have learned thus far. Afterward, I'll share a simple process to determine whether you made money (or not). Let's focus on one of the short-term spreads because one closed early for a profit.

THE COMPLICATED WAY OF DETERMINING PROFIT

I will reference the spread I sold with a November 2024 expiration date. Remember, a credit spread is two simple steps implemented simultaneously. Step 1: I sold an SPX

5730 put and received $10,537.71 in income. Step 2: I took some of the money and bought an SPX 5725 put for $10,370.29. What's left over is a credit of $167.42. That's my potential profit. Right now is an excellent time to test your knowledge. Can you quickly calculate the possible loss and the margin requirement? The answer: Excluding commissions, the potential loss is $330, and the margin requirement was $500.

As I reviewed my transaction history, I saw closing transactions for this credit spread on November 6, 2024. If you subtract the closing values of each put, you get $42.58 ($1,091.29 - $1,048.71). Time decay dwindled the value of the puts. Summary: I sold the options at a high price of $167.42, and now I'm repurchasing them at a cheaper price of $42.58. You subtract those two figures to get my final profit of $124.84.

So that's the complicated way of determining profit: calculating your spread trade's beginning and ending values. You can also download the trades into Excel and have it calculated for you. Finally, closing the spread also frees up the $500 held as a margin requirement. As long as I don't have a losing trade, I can repeatedly use the same $500 to produce more profit for my account. Eventually, even my profit can be recycled and used as a margin requirement for new spreads.

THE SIMPLE WAY OF DETERMINING PROFIT

Each broker will show investments differently, so please research how to understand your broker platform. However, Figure 9 shows what credit spreads look like in my account after I place the trade. When I first sold this spread, I received a credit of $162.42. I could calculate the gain/loss values of $9,145.71 minus $9,058.29 to determine whether it's making money. Doing so, I'd get $87.42; this is the spread's accumulated profit thus far. However, I rarely, if ever, do this. I follow a simple process. I look at the price of SPX ($5,966) and see if it's higher than the strike prices of my puts ($5,800 and $5,805).

Symbol	Name	Qty ↓	Price	% $ Price Chng	Mkt Val	% $ ❶ Day Chng	Cost Basis	% $ ❶ Gain/Loss²
$SPX	S & P 500 INDEX		$5,966.03	+$17.32				
SPX 12/20/2024 5800.00 P ☰∨		1	$31.55	-$8.15	$3,130.00	-$840.00	$12,188.29	-$9,058.29
SPX 12/20/2024 5805.00 P ☰∨		-1	$32.25	-$8.3186	-$3,205.00	+$851.86	-$12,350.71	+$9,145.71

Figure 9: What an SPX put credit spread looks like in my IRA, Source: Schwab.com

As long as SPX is above the strike prices of my credit spread, I know I'm making money on the trade because of time decay. Then, when I log in for my usual once-a-month routine, I look for any credit spreads that closed before their expiration date. It's simple: I made money if my GTC triggered and my trade closed early. No calculations are required.

Remember, I calculate my 2/10 formula at the beginning of the year, and what I can make and lose on each spread is roughly the same throughout the year. So, I know exactly how much I made for every spread that closes early. But again, I'm indifferent about wins and losses. I dollar-cost average, let the stock market do what it does best (go up), and I constantly watch my risk of loss. Sure, I want my account value to go up over time, but usually, when I review my account, I'm ensuring I'm not in a position to lose too much money.

One last recap before we move on: When you sell the spread, the credit is immediately deposited in your account, and your cash balance will increase. However, the broker prevents you from withdrawing the money. They tie it up with the margin requirement. If the trade is a loss, the broker deducts that amount from your account and releases what's left of the margin requirement.

For profitable trades, I sell them, receive a credit, and give back some of that credit to close them early. Said another way, I sell the pair for a credit, then buy back the pair for a debit. When the trade closes for a profit, my account balance will be higher, and my buying power will also increase because the broker frees up the money held as a margin requirement. The alternative to closing them early is to let the spreads expire worthless for 100 percent profit. However, that can be risky because the market could fall, and in that case, you would lose all your profit. I always use GTC orders, but giving up money to close trades early bothers some people. We'll talk about this and more in the next section.

ADDITIONAL MANAGEMENT QUESTIONS

What's the Best Way to Manage a Credit Spread That Goes Against You?

This is the number one question I receive about credit spreads, and it always comes from people who sell high-probability credit spreads. They need to manage their trades because the losses are so significant. Everyone loves high win rates, but a win rate of 90 percent is meaningless if one losing trade wipes out the gains from all the winners. So, the core of this question is, "How can I make money with spreads without giving back all my profit when I have a losing trade?" It's a great question, and I have already answered it. The best way to manage credit spreads is to eliminate the need to manage them. Here's my zero-management approach summarized:

- I stopped selling credit spreads on stocks. It's a hassle and too risky for me.
- I only sell credit spreads on SPX and outsource their management to my broker and GTC orders.
- I also ensure that any loss I take is so small that it doesn't trigger my emotions or destroy my account. I accomplish that by selling six- to twelve-month at-the-money credit spreads and following the 2/10 formula.

You may struggle with my zero-management approach if you have been brainwashed to believe that out-of-the-money credit spreads on stocks are superior. But don't knock it until you try it. Finally, I'll leave you with a quote:

> *Should you find yourself in a chronically leaking boat, energy devoted to changing vessels is likely to be more productive than energy devoted to patching leaks.*
>
> — WARREN BUFFETT

High-probability out-of-the-money credit spreads are a crappy strategy with a crappy risk/reward. Instead of using a strategy that requires complicated management techniques, just change vessels. It's what I did, and Buffett was right—it was more productive. I stopped selling high-probability spreads on stocks and switched to long-term at-the-money spreads on SPX. It was one of the best financial decisions of my life. Now, I feel sorry for all the people who blow out their accounts with the conventional approach to selling spreads.

Why Don't You Roll Your Spreads or Manage Them to Try and Prevent Losses?

This is a variation of the previous question, but answering it allows me to rant more (I'm smiling as I write this).

Rolling is a technique out-of-the-money spread traders use to fix bad trades. They try to make up for the huge losses by selling new spreads. Sorry, I'm not interested in trying to fix a crappy approach to selling spreads. Also, I have not found a way to roll spreads while maintaining or lowering the risk of loss.

Usually, to roll spreads, you must increase your risk even higher to compensate for the loss you just took. Yeah, no thanks! Increasing your potential loss is not a smart way to get rich. I rarely lose on DCA credit spreads, so I don't manage or roll them. Also, I've structured things on the front end with the 2/10 formula so that any loss I take is not financially devasting. That formula is how I protect myself, ensuring these little extra income trades don't hurt me. They can only really help me.

I also don't fear losing money because my risk of loss is defined upfront. I always know the worst-case scenario: losing 10 percent of my account. For that to happen, I'd have to have five to six losing trades in a row, which means the market fell and never recovered. This tends to occur in a bear market, and it did happen to my trades during the bear market of 2022. So, let's put real numbers to this: If I have a $10,000 account and lose $1,000 on credit spreads, I have $9,000 left. Can I quickly recoup the $1K loss with the $9K? Yes, I can. Thus, I don't need to roll my losing trades.

Finally, here are my blunt thoughts about losing money. Trying to avoid taking losses is like going to a swimming pool and trying to avoid getting wet. It's unrealistic. The reality is that losing money is a part of all successful investing. Think about your favorite successful investor. Do you have their name in your mind? If so, they lose money, too. If they can still succeed despite losing money, that should tell you that losing money is not a big deal. It's not something that will hold you back from success.

Ultimately, you're selling insurance, and no insurance business makes money all the time. They factor losses into the equation. Since we are dollar-cost averaging into the market, our wins should be greater than our losses. So stop being a scaredy-cat and learn how to manage your risk prudently. On that note, selling far out-of-the-money credit spreads is not a prudent way of managing risk. Instead of using a broken strategy that requires rolling and has you terrified of losing money, try the simple long-term, at-the-money, zero-management approach taught in this book.

If Closing Spreads Early Costs You Money, Why Don't You Just Let Them Expire Worthless?

I often encounter people who struggle with the fact that I leave profit on the table by closing my spreads early with GTC orders. Sometimes, I forfeit a few hundred dollars in profit, but in larger accounts, you will leave thousands on the table. It seems like an irresponsible financial decision, but let me share how I explained it to my wife. She usually sells a six-month duration credit spread and, on average, receives a $1,400 credit. Her GTC order will forfeit roughly $300 in profit in exchange for closing the trade early. Since the market rises over time, her spread will likely achieve 80 percent of its profit in only three months.

When she had her first profitable trade, we had this conversation: "You made $1,100 in three months. You have a guaranteed profit you can take right now. Do you want to wait another three months to earn the remaining $300?" No one likes giving up money for no reason, so the greed in her will say yes. Also, when greed is present, you rarely consider the potential risk of losing money. Therefore, I explained to her what could also happen: "Keep in mind that the market could fall. Are you willing to lose $1,100 in profit to make a measly $300?" When I ask this way, the answer is always no. I also reminded her that by closing the trade early, she could free up the margin to place another trade and, hopefully, make another $1,100 in three months. So, she could potentially make $2,200 in six months versus waiting for the entire duration of the initial trade.

But what if the second trade is a loser? If that happens, she's essentially back to breakeven because the profit from the first trade offset the loss on the second trade. In summary: Don't be greedy! When I sell a credit spread, I put in a GTC order to close it once it has achieved 80 percent of its maximum profit. When the market blesses me with a quick profit, I will take it because I can't predict the future. A guaranteed 80 percent profit is better than losing it because I was too greedy. Closing profitable trades early is another way we manage the risk of the unknown. The other ways you are already familiar with are selling long-term spreads, risking 2 percent of our account, etc.

Do You Immediately Sell Another Credit Spread if You Use a GTC and Have a Spread Close Early?

No, I don't. I want to control my routine; I don't want the stock market to control me. I also want to systemize how I make money, so I use a dollar-cost average approach and show up once a month to sell my spreads. Again, "when" you sell them in the month is not essential. It's the consistency of showing up that is vital.

However, I make one exception to my "once-a-month" routine: If the market falls 5, 10, or 15 percent, I will sell new credit spreads at each price point to take advantage of the lower price. I don't wait until the end of the month; I sell a spread as soon as it hits those price levels. Also, here's a secret bonus tip: Market corrections are often when I sell in-the-money credit spreads because I get a slightly better risk/reward. So, instead of selling an ATM spread, I sell a long-term credit spread that is maybe 1 to

3 percent higher than the stock price. Of course, with these bonus trades, I ensure I stay within the risk parameters of the 2/10 formula. If the market falls, but my risk is already maxed out, I don't place any new trades (no matter how tempting it is). Managing risk is your #1 job.

If the Market Falls Below the 200-DMA and You Have Trades Open, Do You Close Them?

Some people close theirs because it eases their emotions and makes them feel better. If it happens to be a short dip and the market rises above the 200-DMA shortly after, you can always re-open the same trades or start new ones. However, I usually don't close mine. If the market falls below its 200-day average, most of my spreads will be at max loss, and I see no reason to close them. Again, I sell SPX credit spreads, so there is no risk of stock assignment. I also don't want to invest the time to close them. I let the broker handle losing trades for me.

Also, my odd mental quirk is that when I sell credit spreads, I assume I will lose on the trade. I know it's weird, but I do this to manage my emotions, and it helps me not be sloppy with my risk. Thus, when I have a loss, it's not a big deal as I prepared for it. However, if the trade is profitable, it's a happy surprise. The reverse is also true. Anytime I place a trade, assuming it will work out, I tend to get super crabby if it turns into a loss.

What Are Your Average Days in Trade for Long-Term Spreads?

I don't know, and I don't care. It's not a metric I track because it's primarily based on the movement of the stock market. My primary focus with my account is managing the risk of loss, something I can control. That said, I can confidently say that my spread trades rarely, if ever, stay open for their entire duration. I primarily sell six-month spreads, and my most recent one closed within three months. But again, it's not something I pay attention to. I mainly focus on risk and leave the rest to the stock market.

Also, I'm an experienced investor, so my results may not match yours. However, my wife is a beginner investor, so here is a small sample from her account. In May 2024, she sold an SPX credit spread with a December 2024 expiration. That spread closed for a profit on November 6th. In June 2024, she sold an SPX credit spread with a January 2025 expiration. That spread closed for a profit on November 13th. We generally have a spread close every month, but the average days in trade are variable and highly dependent on the movement of the stock market.

You Didn't Talk About What Delta You Choose, Widening
the Width of the Spreads Strikes, or Even Open Interest. Am
I Missing Something?

Nope, you're not missing anything. I didn't talk about that because it's unimportant to me. It's not a part of my process. All that would have been important if I were a trader, but I'm not anymore. I'm a buy-and-hold investor who uses options to enhance my returns. Thus, I stick to a simple process and eliminate the unnecessary complexity of options trading. However, I won't stop you if you want to geek out on those topics.

12

MISCELLANEOUS CREDIT SPREAD QUESTIONS

> *You don't have to be great to start, but you have to start to be great.*
>
> — ZIG ZIGLAR

If you want to become good at making money with credit spreads, I highly suggest you read this book two to three times. I also encourage you to implement the concepts learned; don't procrastinate by accumulating more information. At this point, you have a "good enough" understanding of credit spreads and should be able to place trades yourself. However, for some, their fearful mind will convince them they can't act unless they obtain more information. That is not true; you learn more by doing. Regardless, I want to spend some time answering a few additional questions I received from those new to my method of selling spreads.

I Have Less than $10,000. Can I Still Sell Credit Spreads?

Yes, you can, but if you have a small account, the challenge you will face is not the ability to generate passive income but your emotions. The income produced on a smaller account will be a few hundred dollars a month. That amount is usually not enough to make a meaningful impact in your life. Thus, I encourage you to consider account growth your priority, not income. My book, *10-Minute Options Trading and ETF Investing*, will teach you how to grow a small account into a six-figure account.

However, this book is about income, so if you have a smaller account and want to sell options for income, you can consider selling credit spreads on XSP, the mini version of the S&P 500 index. It's another index option that offers the same benefits as SPX. The one negative is that XSP has a lower trading volume, but in my experience, this does not hinder profit. Once your account surpasses $10,000, you can slowly transition to selling SPX credit spreads, as the account should be able to handle the higher risk of loss. There are other index options you can research to sell credit spreads on, but SPX and XSP are the only two I have experience with.

Can I Use Credit Spreads to Grow My Account Fast?

Put credit spreads are usually not the best strategy for growing accounts because your profit is capped or limited to the income received upfront. No matter how high the stock market rises, you can't make more than the spread's maximum profit. Buying stocks or options would be better for account growth. Also, no matter how many people get upset with me, I'll keep saying this. Your account balance will not skyrocket until you accept this sobering truth: **No options strategy can "consistently" grow a small account "fast." None!** High savings + prudent investing + compounding is the best way to super-size your portfolio.

You can try to grow a small account by investing alone, but it will take forever. For example, $2,000, which earns 24 percent a year for ten years, grows into $17,000. Twenty-four percent each year for ten years is hard for most, and only having $17K after ten years is disappointing. However, if you deposit $550 into the account monthly, that same $2,000, earning "only" 10 percent a year, grows to $110,000! This is a much lower return and nearly five times as much money. If you want a large account, you know what to do. Get busy earning and saving more income in any legal way you can. Sell stuff, get another job, start a business, do what you must.

How Can I Get Rich If I Risk Only 2 Percent of My Account on Each Trade and Leave 90 Percent in Cash?

You don't have to keep 90 percent of your money in cash. I don't. My 90 percent is invested in the S&P 500. The 2/10 formula is based on all of my stock market investments, and it's just a way of ensuring that I manage my risk of loss with this one strategy. However, I'll use my wife's account as an example because it only has credit spreads. She was fortunate to have no losing trades in 2024 despite the market having three corrections. And this was all because she sold long-term credit spreads. The market fell and recovered in price before the spread expired.

Of course, we fully expect to have losses in the future, which will bring our average down. But imagine if each of those credit spreads grew her account by 2 percent. That would be a 24 percent return for the year. That return means nothing to my wife as she's not a fan of math, but consistently earning 24 percent a year can help you get rich faster than most. And you could have earned that by keeping most of your account in cash, protected from a market crash. Again, I don't keep my 90 percent in cash, but people who only use this strategy often do.

Finally, let's talk about losses. The prudent 2/10 formula approach is why I succeeded and am investing after 25 years. Many others have lost all their money because they focused on getting rich. Put more bluntly, when it comes to options trading, **there are more crash-and-burn stories than rags-to-riches stories!** The secret to why that is has been indirectly sprinkled throughout this book. I hope you received the message: Don't be an idiot, don't be greedy, and don't "*try*" to get rich. Instead, attract wealth by being a prudent investor who stewards money. If you abuse your money by gambling with it, don't be surprised when your money runs into the arms of someone who will show it more love and respect.

Regardless, the best chance of getting rich is to ensure you never have an account-crippling loss. Believe it or not, this is something you have control over. There are no innocent victims in the stock market, only people who put themselves in a position to lose a lot of money. The stock market historically goes up more than it goes down, so if you protect yourself from losing a lot of money during the occasional market decline, the gains take care of themselves. At least, that has been my experience thus far. However, I have no idea what your results will be, nor can I guarantee you will be able to achieve my returns. You may do worse, or you may do better.

I Know We'll Win Some Months, Lose Some Months, and Not Place A Trade Some Months, But What Might the Average Annual Income Be with a $50,000 Account?

My mentor called this a "theory question" and advised me not to ask them because they don't put money in your pocket. He encouraged me to ask implementation questions. Those are questions that surface as you are implementing a new strategy. For instance, the best way to know what "you" will earn on $50K is to keep showing up and implementing the cash flow blueprint. In my experience, your performance is based mainly on your habits and how you think. It's not dependent on the blueprint because I've seen two people use it—one succeeded, and the other failed. The person who failed couldn't overcome their fear, greed, and worry about what the market may do next.

I've been selling credit spreads now for almost twenty years. My performance has been all over the place because it depends on the stock market. That said, I conservatively estimate that I'll earn (on average) 1 to 2 percent a month in the long run. So, with a $50,000 account, I would expect to generate $500 to $1,000 in monthly income. Sometimes, I earn more, and sometimes less, but 1 to 2 percent is what I mentally prepare for. Ultimately, I show up, implement the blueprint, and get what I get. More often than not, I'm happy with the performance I get.

How Do You Structure an Account to Generate $50,000 to $100,000 Yearly?

Oddly enough, I don't set income targets anymore. When I tried in the past, it never worked. I can set out to make $50,000 a year, but the stock market doesn't care about my goals. Trying to force an uncontrollable entity to give me a set amount of money leads to emotional investing. What I make in any given year is highly dependent on the stock market, so I cannot control it. Now, I show up, implement the four simple steps already shared, and leave my performance up to chance. I focus only on the things I can control.

However, to answer the question, estimating yearly income is easier once you have years of experience managing your money. You divide your target annual earnings by the average returns you achieve. For example, if you need $50,000 and, on average, generate 15 percent a year with credit spreads, you know you need to accumulate a $333,000 portfolio ($50K ÷ 0.15). With that account, you'd follow the cash flow blueprint to generate consistent income in up markets. One last but crucial point: People underestimate how they will emotionally handle a bear market. So, this average return should include at least one bear market.

Why Not Sell Credit Spreads That Expire Each Week to Earn More (Weekly Options)?

This question assumes that selling weekly options will increase one's income. Many investors get so excited about the income potential of credit spreads that they try to get paid every week. In theory, the more trades a person places, the more they can make, but it rarely works out that way. Also, I'm teaching a passive income system. Don't make the mistake of turning this process into another full-time job. Speaking of jobs, in a business, who earns the most money, the hard-working employees or the CEO? Usually, the CEO, even though the employees do most of the work. So when you start selling credit spreads, I want you to channel your inner CEO.

Another point. You may struggle with this ten-minute, once-a-month routine if you grew up poor or middle class. You've been taught that the more you work, the more you can make. However, the opposite is often true for wealthy people. Also, it will initially feel uncomfortable making lots of money without doing much "work." Especially as you observe those around you work much harder for less money. You may even feel guilty; at least I did. I even talked to a money coach about it.

Ultimately, you must be willing to sit in the discomfort of making lots of money without much effort until it becomes your new reality. Try to resist any temptation to trade more frequently. Over time, your emotions will adjust, and you will grow to enjoy passive investing. More importantly, the complicated, time-intensive approaches others teach will no longer interest you, assuming you're not a high IQ person who likes stimulating their brain. I've noticed that really smart people always screw up my simple system and make it more complicated than it needs to be.

Why Do You Only Trade Once a Month?

I trade once a month because I want to generate passive income, not active income. Also, a millionaire once told me I was attracted to active trading because of my working-class mentality. He, not so kindly, pointed out how he made more money than me yet worked less. He also taught me a valuable lesson about financial leverage: making the most money with the least physical effort. He showed me that the less time I spend managing my portfolio, the higher my hourly pay rate will be.

For instance, the high-probability credit spread approach is time-intensive. Imagine I make $200K a year with that approach and spend five hours a week managing my portfolio. That's a $769 per hour pay rate. Most would love to get paid this much, but here is one that's better.

Compare that to the four-step passive income blueprint. I show up once a month to place a long-term, dollar-cost average credit spread. If I make $100K yearly as a passive options investor and spend two hours a year (ten minutes a month), that equals a $50,000 per hour pay rate. Yes, I made half as much money, but my hourly pay rate is higher. And I gained more free time, which is priceless.

Why Do You Only Invest in SPY or SPX?

In my second book, *10-Minute Options Trading and ETF Investing*, I devoted an entire chapter to this question.

However, the summary is that low-cost index funds are a great way to invest passively in the stock market. Even Warren Buffett has said that for most Americans, investing in these low-cost index funds is the best way to grow their wealth over time (Locke 2022). As a savvy investor, I can handle a complicated stock strategy and would do fine. However, I won't live forever, and I don't want my wife to inherit a big mess of confusion that she has no idea what to do with.

Now, we follow a one-stock retirement plan. The S&P 500 has become the ultimate "set-it-and-forget-it" stock we can hold forever and even pass down to our kids. More importantly, the S&P has listed options to trade, which means we can obtain growth, income, and market crash protection with just one stock. It's the trifecta of wealth building, and for us, there are more pros than cons to using this one stock blueprint. It's also the simplest path to wealth I have ever encountered. I see no need to invest in anything else. So, please don't email me to ask what I think about your favorite stock. You do you. As for me and my house, we are 100 percent S&P.

Is There Ever a Time You Sell Shorter-Term Spreads?

I generally sell long-term at-the-money spreads that expire six to twelve months in the future. It's a counterintuitive approach to selling short-term spreads. Here's what I mean: a sixty-day spread used to be a 180-day spread. Put another way, my long-term spreads eventually turn into short-term spreads. For example, if you look at my account, I have short-term spreads that expire anywhere from thirty to sixty days from today. However, they had six to twelve months until expiration when I first sold them.

But to specifically answer the question, yes, after the market has fallen 5 to 10 percent, I am willing to sell a short-term at-the-money spread that expires in sixty to ninety days. The risk for shorter-term spreads is the market falling, so I prefer not to sell them when the market is at all-time highs. If the market has already fallen, that risk is minimized. However, the market could keep falling, and that's where the 2/10 formula protects me.

How Might the Election Season Affect Your Thinking (Or Fill in the Blank with Whatever "Event" You're Worried About)?

I prefer not to make assumptions about how an event will affect the stock market. The future is too unpredictable, so I like to plan for the best and fully prepare for the worst. For instance, I plan on living a long life but bought life insurance in case I don't. Regarding my investments, the election season does not affect my thinking or routine. The stock market goes up, down, or sideways. That's a fact, and no election or world event has changed that fact.

And since I know how to make money in up, down, and sideways markets, I see no reason to stress about presidential elections.

This question also demonstrates something I stated earlier in the book: Strategy and mindset are the keys to success. I've taught others this credit spread method, and they don't do as well as I do. We have the same strategy, so our results should be identical, but they aren't. They have different mental hurdles than I do. I show up and implement like a robot, giving little thought to what's happening in the world or who's running the country. Others worry about those things, and it affects their decisions. Sometimes, they hesitate and don't sell spreads because of fear. I show up, have fear, but push forward anyway. I'm not bragging; I'm just trying to demonstrate how strategy alone is not the key to success.

What Do You Do with Your Profits or the Cash You Add to Your Account?

Almost everyone I talk to shares the same sentiment: *I don't want to leave a lot of money sitting in cash.* When I inquire further, the reason is often the fear of missing out on potential profit. This is a common bias: the belief that investing cash will always yield positive returns. However, it's important to remember that there's also a chance of losing money once the cash is invested. Again, successful investors focus on risk first and profits second.

I view cash as a defensive investment, meaning that I view lots of cash as a good thing, not a bad thing. I use my cash to take advantage of market corrections and crashes. It's also dependent on "how much" cash I have. For instance, when we sold one of our rental properties, we immediately invested the money into the S&P 500 via enhanced buy-and-hold (the strategy taught in my second book). However, with smaller amounts of money, I'm okay with leaving it uninvested until the annual rebalance of my portfolio, when I will put it to work.

Do You Also Sell Covered Calls for Income?

Note to beginners: This book is only about credit spreads, but I'm answering this because I mentioned this strategy in my second book. An oversimplified explanation of covered calls: It's how you can rent out your stock shares for income. You buy a stock and sell call options against it, giving people the opportunity to buy your shares from you. It's similar to buying a house and doing a lease-to-own rental contract.

Now, to answer the question. No, I don't sell covered calls, but I used to. They don't align with the estate plan we created. After both of my parents passed away, we did our estate plan and realized that since I was the only one who managed the money, we were screwed if anything happened to me. Scenario: I pass away, my covered call is exercised, and my shares are called away (sold).

Meanwhile, my wife is busy grieving, planning a funeral, and managing life after I'm gone. She thinks we are invested but doesn't realize that most of our money is in cash.

Essentially, covered calls are an active trading strategy that requires active management. We set up our investments so that if I pass away, the compounding of our accounts will not be interrupted. I miss the income from covered calls but use credit spreads to compensate for the lost revenue. If my wife ever decides to learn how to sell covered calls, I may start using them again. However, I'm not sure because buy-and-hold has spoiled me.

Do You Sell Credit Spreads with Enhanced Buy-and-Hold or Keep Them in a Separate Account?

In a later bonus chapter, I'll share how I integrate credit spreads with enhanced buy-and-hold. However, we have a separate account in which we only sell credit spreads. It's my wife's spending account, which I referred to earlier. Here is a snapshot of her current positions, including the March 2025 SPX credit spread you saw at the beginning of the book. Of course, she and the kids followed the same simple four-step process shared earlier in the book.

Symbol ↓	Name	Qty	Price	% $ Price Chng	Mkt Val	% $ ❶ Day Chng	Cost Basis	% $ ❶ Gain/Loss[2]
$SPX	S & P 500 INDEX		$5,893.18	+$22.56				
SPX 02/21/2025 5525.00 P ☰ˇ		2	$53.90	-$7.4056	$10,780.00	-$1,481.12	$36,636.58	-70.58%
SPX 02/21/2025 5550.00 P ☰ˇ		-2	$56.85	-$7.7176	-$11,370.00	+$1,543.52	-$38,141.42	+70.19%
SPX 03/21/2025 5550.00 P ☰ˇ		1	$74.40	-$8.20	$7,455.00	-$805.00	$17,463.29	-57.31%
SPX 03/21/2025 5600.00 P ☰ˇ		-1	$81.85	-$8.55	-$8,180.00	+$860.00	-$18,880.71	+56.68%
SPX 04/17/2025 5625.00 P ☰ˇ		2	$101.35	﹩9.05	$20,280.00	-$1,800.00	$41,390.58	-51%
SPX 04/17/2025 5650.00 P ☰ˇ		-2	$105.85	-$9.2211	-$21,160.00	+$1,854.22	-$42,885.42	+50.66%
SPX 05/16/2025 5825.00 P ☰ˇ		2	$161.35	-$11.20	$32,260.00	-$2,250.00	$40,540.58	-20.43%
SPX 05/16/2025 5850.00 P ☰ˇ		-2	$168.05	-$11.50	-$33,600.00	+$2,310.00	-$41,985.42	+19.97%
Total Indices					**-$3,535.00**	**+$231.62**	**-$5,861.94**	**+39.7%**

Figure 10: A snapshot of my wife's credit spread portfolio, Source: Schwab.com

If you're new to credit spreads, I want you to ignore how busy and complicated the account looks. I'll summarize it because a lot is happening in the photo, and it may be hard to read. I only want you to focus on two things: the price of the S&P 500 and the strike prices of her spreads. At the time of this snapshot, the S&P 500 was trading at $5,893. The strike prices of her four credit spread positions range from $5525 to $5850. In other words, the S&P 500 is above all her credit spreads, and she is benefiting from the time decay of the options.

Remember, this is an insurance trade. She sold insurance and will make money if no one files an insurance claim (exercises the put). That won't happen if the S&P stays where it's at or moves higher in price. She will make money if the price of the S&P 500 stays above the strike prices of the spreads she sold, and she'll lose money if it doesn't. Put credit spreads don't need stock movement to profit; they need the stock to stay above the puts you sell. Credit spreads can be difficult to understand initially, but that simple explanation summarizes how easy it is to profit from these insurance trades.

Finally, my wife and kids follow a 50/50 formula for withdrawing money: Spend 50 percent of their income and save 50 percent. When they sell a spread each month, they review previous trades to see if any are closed for a profit. If so, they withdraw half of their earnings and leave the other half in the account to compound and grow larger. If they took a loss, there is nothing to withdraw, so they'd return next month and repeat the process. Now, let's move on so I can share how I integrate credit spreads with the enhanced buy-and-hold blueprint.

BONUS

ENHANCED BUY-AND-HOLD INCOME

> *Successful people do what unsuccessful people are not willing to do. Don't wish it were easier; wish you were better.*
>
> — JIM ROHN

I am adding this bonus chapter to reward those who read my second book, *10-Minute Options Trading and ETF Investing.* If you have not read that book, I hope you still find some value in this chapter, but it's probably best to read it first. In that book, I share the core foundation of my approach to investing: I'm a buy-and-hold investor who uses options to enhance my returns. You'll also hear the inspiring story of Sam and Sara. Two ordinary, hard-working people who used enhanced buy-and-hold (EBH) to grow their five-figure investment account to nearly half a million dollars. This amount allowed Sara to retire early.

I'm also sharing this because I anticipate someone will want to know how to integrate credit spreads with the enhanced buy-and-hold strategy taught in that book. You'll learn all that and more in this chapter, but let's start with a quick refresher on enhanced buy-and-hold. An EBH portfolio consists of the following:

1. Shares of a broad-based ETF or index fund for safe and stable returns
2. Put options for peace of mind and stock market insurance
3. Call options to pay for the puts and potentially boost the account's profit

It's a relatively simple blueprint that takes me ten minutes once a year to set up and produces above-average returns over three to five years (your results will vary). That said, after I shared my market-beating blueprint, two groups emerged: those who implemented enhanced buy-and-hold and those who didn't. Those who did not implement it would frequently ask, "How do I generate income with EBH?" Those who did implement it rarely, if ever, ask that question. I believe they never asked because they discovered the same thing I did regarding income and profit.

PROFIT IS INCOME, AND INCOME IS PROFIT

I wrote this book to provide people with a specific strategy they could use for income, but I want to explain why it's not as important as people think. With enhanced buy-and-hold, we buy options to grow our accounts quickly. With the cash flow strategy, we sell options to earn consistent income. These are two entirely different strategies, each with its own set of pros and cons. However, let's assume they both produce the same investment results in one year.

- Investor A implements EBH with a $50,000 account and grows the portfolio by 20% in one year. During the annual rebalance, they have a chance to withdraw cash.
- Investor B sells put credit spreads with a $50,000 account and grows the portfolio by 20% in one year. They can withdraw their profits as soon as the trades close.
- Both accounts produced $10,000 in profit—one with an option-buying strategy and one with an option-selling strategy.

If I go to a store to spend my EBH profits, they don't say, "You didn't get this income from selling credit spreads; we can't take it." My sarcastic point is that the money can be spent the same whether you profit from option buying or selling. It makes little difference what strategy you use to create the money, but that's what I think. This book is about you, and you may disagree with my philosophy or have counterarguments, so let me share three income methods you can use with enhanced buy-and-hold.

Traditional Buy-and-Hold Income

I discussed what we do for EBH income in my second book, but it's easy to miss as it's only a few sentences long. If we ever need to withdraw money from our enhanced buy-and-hold portfolio, we use the excess option profits or sell some of our stock shares. Another option is to spend the dividends the stock shares produce. This is no different from what traditional buy-and-hold investors do when they need income. However, with the credit spread income tweak, you can withdraw money without interrupting the growth of your stock shares.

Credit Spread Income

I've implemented this in my family account and will add a few examples of my credit spreads to the book bonus webpage. Let's start with the classic EBH setup and how one might add credit spreads to the mix. Here is the classic EBH setup that follows the 80/20 wealth-building formula:

- 100 shares of SPY bought at $468 a share
- 1 SPY 540-strike call option bought for $4,330

- 1 SPY 540-strike put option bought for $7,578
- **Total Investment:** $58,708

The only way the above profits is if the stock market rises in price. However, with credit spreads, you can make money in sideways markets. Here is enhanced buy-and-hold with the income tweak (EBHI):

- 100 shares of SPY bought at $468 a share
- 1 SPY 540-strike call option bought for $4,330
- 1 SPY 540-strike put option bought for $7,578
- 1-5 low-risk put credit spreads that generate an estimated $500 to $1,000 monthly

Roughly $1,000 to $5,000 extra is needed in the account to handle the margin requirement of any spreads I wish to sell. However, I can always sell a few stock shares to raise money if I don't have it. If I were setting up a new portfolio, I'd subtract $5,000 from my starting amount of $58,000. That amount would be left in cash to satisfy the margin requirement of any spreads I sell. With the $53K left over, I would set up my EBH portfolio. Also, with spreads in the portfolio, roughly 75 percent of your money is allocated to buy-and-hold, and 25 percent is allocated to option positions. That's close enough to 80/20 and is still relatively safe because most of your money is in the safest asset: broad-based ETFs or index funds.

EBH Versus EBHI

If you've implemented enhanced buy-and-hold, you know credit spreads are unnecessary. The EBH blueprint works just fine without the credit spread tweak. The extra income earned from buying options can be spent the same way as option-selling income. However, EBHI's one benefit is that it allows you to earn a steady income without interrupting the massive compounding of the core blueprint. When you pair credit spreads with enhanced buy-and-hold, you create a powerful combination of rapidly building wealth and generating consistent monthly income. Implementing both strategies is also not a huge time commitment.

You rebalance your EBH investments once a year, and then, once a month, if the conditions are safe, you spend a few minutes selling a credit spread for passive income. Believe it or not, that's my entire investment process, neatly wrapped in one sentence. For the record, placing my monthly spread trade takes me roughly five minutes. However, my wife takes about fifteen minutes to implement alone and thirty minutes with the kids because of all the sibling bickering. Regardless, that simple process allows us to earn enough to pay our bills while still having enough free time to enjoy life and give back to society. And if you're among the many thinking, *Hold up, it can't be that easy. You spend ten minutes once a year, then a few minutes once a month clicking buttons and* *bringing in thousands from selling options. What am I missing?*

It is simple, and I am baffled why so many people make investing so complicated. However, simple does not mean easy. It takes a lot of discipline and humility to be okay with a childlike ten-minute investing process that produces above-average market returns. Ego and arrogance will always tempt you to find complicated answers to simple problems.

Regarding what you're missing, it's probably the nearly thirty years of experience that went into this process. When you're new, you don't know what's important or not, so everything seems important. But I have enough experience to identify the essentials and eliminate the rest. I reduced my investment process to a simple ten-minute routine by eliminating the unnecessary. Some people know this as Pareto's principle: 80 percent of your results come from 20 percent of your efforts. I eliminated the 80 percent and only focused on the 20 percent that produced the biggest profits. Finally, let me end with another income tweak I was extremely hesitant about mentioning in this book.

BONUS: THE NAKED PUT TWEAK (FOR EXPERIENCED PUT-SELLERS ONLY)

I'm ending with the riskiest income tweak, selling naked put options. This is a bonus within a bonus chapter because naked puts are not the book's core focus. The strategy is also too dangerous to detail in print, so I'd like to begin with a few warnings. Please ignore this section if you don't have at least ten years of successful put-selling experience or a mentor to walk you through selling uncovered puts. If you don't know what I mean by naked puts, definitely skip this section.

Really, I'm not kidding. I estimate that most option failure stories come from people who engage in naked option strategies. Naked option strategies are how many lose all their money and go bankrupt. Also, if you don't understand the following option gibberish, you're not ready for this approach (yet). And trust me, you don't want to be in a rush; I cannot over-emphasize how dangerous this approach is.

With all of that out of the way, let's begin. I am only sharing this tweak because 1) you are now familiar with selling put options, and 2) it was mentioned in my second book. In that book, I discuss how Sam and Sara sold out-of-the-money options against their stock insurance, known as calendar spreads. They can do this in their retirement account because of how EBH is structured. Usually, when you sell puts inside a retirement account, the broker requires you to have the total amount needed in case the put is exercised.

So, if I sold a 540-strike put option in a retirement account, the broker would require me to have $54,000 cash. Again, this is what is known as a margin requirement. However, if I sold a 540-strike put against the above EBH portfolio, the margin requirement would be zero dollars. That's right, I could sell puts without any margin requirement. This is possible because the broker views the sold put as part of a calendar spread.

The broker "thinks" the put I sold is covered by the put I bought to protect my stock shares. Of course, that's not the case, so I view this as a naked put. I legitimately don't have the money to buy stock shares if the put I sold is exercised. If the stock falls in price, my naked put will lose a sickening amount of money! And if I'm unlucky and the put I sold is exercised, I will get nasty letters from my broker demanding I deposit more money. If I don't transfer more money, they can liquidate my account. Didn't I tell you this is a risky strategy?

But why do people like Sam and Sara use it if it's so risky? They do so because rolling or adjusting puts is a way to manage the assignment risk. Again, this is not the book's core focus, and this lesson is only for experienced put-sellers. But the summary is that Sam and Sara sold out-of-the-money puts against their EBH portfolio. If the market fell in price, they repurchased the puts for a massive loss and sold new puts that brought in so much money that it offset the loss. In other words, they rolled the puts "out in time" and "down in price" to avoid the assignment risk.

Am I suggesting you do this? Heck no! If you're a new investor and don't want to lose a lot of money, I suggest you avoid naked option strategies. Again, it's one of the frequent ways people go broke. People tend to get greedy and usually blow up their accounts if they don't have someone to hold them accountable.

Selling long-term at-the-money credit spreads is a <u>much</u> safer income strategy because the maximum you can lose is capped at a small amount. Also, EBH already allows me to outperform the market. I have no reason to try and get even more greedy with naked puts. That said, I can neither confirm nor deny that I occasionally sell naked puts. All jokes aside, here are two guidelines I follow if I sell naked puts.

- I don't get greedy.
- I don't let my naked puts ever come close to being assigned. I closely monitor the time or extrinsic value of my naked puts.

I've been early assigned on naked puts a lot! The one thing they all had in common was a time value of less than $1. This makes sense because if an option has too much time value built into its price, it's not advantageous for the put's owner to exercise it. The one challenge with naked puts is that they pose a significant risk to my portfolio if the market crashes and I'm not around to roll the options. Thus, if I ever sell one, I inform my wife about it first, and then I aim to be super conservative. I would only target an extra 3 percent on my portfolio a year.

For example, if I have a $50,000 account, I'm perfectly fine with a small naked put profit of $1,500 for the year. That's an average of only $125 a month and is very doable. I can achieve that by selling an out-of-the-money put each month or one long-term out-of-the-money put each year. However, some newbie investors are what I call profit snobs. They scoff and turn their nose up at the small dollar amounts until I show them that small dollar amounts can add up over time.

- $50,000, earning 12% annually for twenty years, grows into $482,314.
- $50,000, earning 15% annually for twenty years, grows into $818,326.

You don't get rich by turning away money! If $1,500 in relatively passive income doesn't excite you, let me send you my mailing address so you can mail me that amount each year. I'll gladly take it if you're too good for the money. Teasing aside, let me share the EBHI system so you can visually see how we earn multiple income streams from one stock.

EBHI PERFORMANCE ESTIMATES

Please note: The performance will vary yearly because it depends on the stock market; these are rough estimates. In any given year, these numbers could be higher or even lower.

- I buy shares of the S&P 500 primarily for growth and secondarily for passive income via dividends. This can generate an average annual return of 9 to 15% on my account.
- I buy put options primarily to insure my stock shares and secondarily for peace of mind. This <u>cost me</u>, on average, a negative 5 to 9% of my account each year.
- I buy call options primarily to pay for my puts and secondarily to boost my income. This can generate an average annual return of 7 to 15% on my account.
- I sell put credit spreads primarily for income and secondarily for account growth. This can generate an average annual return of 7 to 10% on my account.
- I sell naked put options, primarily for a small drip of income, but it <u>must</u> be managed. This can generate, on average, a 2 to 3% return on my account each year. Bonus tip: I use this income for credit spread margin to avoid pulling money from my EBH strategy.

First, I'd like to point out why the credit spread return is slightly lower than the examples shown at the beginning of the book. I am more aggressive if I have an account that only sells credit spreads since most of that account is in cash (2/10 formula). However, if I pair credit spreads with EBH, I may only risk 0.5 to 1 percent of my account on each credit spread. Could I try to earn more? Sure, but being greedy has never worked out for me.

Instead, I lower my risk so that no one strategy can ruin me financially. For instance, if the stock market falls 50 percent like it did during the 2007-2009 bear market, here is what I can expect.

- I'd lose 10% of my account value due to the call option loss.
- I'd lose 10% of my account value to the credit spread loss.
- My stock shares would be down 50%.
- However, the puts I bought for insurance would be profitable. They'd offset roughly 45% of my stock share loss.

The naked puts would lose almost as much as the stock shares, but that loss would be offset and pushed out in time via rolling. So, even in a 50 percent market decline, my account's loss would be capped at around 25 to 30 percent. In my experience, the way to make more money is to keep your overall losses smaller than your gains.

Speaking of gains, most people view the above as a complicated mix of "strategies." However, I view it as five ways to profit from one stock, and it's the secret to my high performance. It is much superior to traditional buy-and-hold, where you only make money in two ways: stock appreciation and dividends. With each strategy I add, my performance increases, and my losses are capped. Best of all, it legitimately takes me ten minutes once a year to set up and a few minutes each month to sell a spread. Finally, the total "average" yearly return, including the insurance cost, is 20 to 34 percent (your results will vary).

That return is ridiculously high, and I want to be crystal clear: I never try to beat the stock market. I buy the "market" (S&P 500), and because I pair it up with options, I often get higher returns than average. The growth can be even better if someone adds money to their account. For example, if you start with $25,000, add $550 to the account each month and generate an average return of 28 percent annually for ten years. Your account will grow to $549,858, and with credit spreads alone, you could generate a passive income of $3,200 to $5,400 a month. Sadly, though, a person with a loser's limp won't even try to achieve this. They will whine that my return estimates are too high and that no one can possibly earn that consistently. They might also complain that they don't have $25,000.

However, people without that sickening self-limitation would ask themselves, *How can I save $25,000 as quickly as* *possible?* And since they are not acting like a whiny victim, they will also understand that I'm not promising you can achieve this. However, if you want to see what's possible and potentially make this your reality, you know what to do: Trust but verify. Before you do that, though, I have a few parting thoughts.

FINAL THOUGHTS

 Simplicity is the ultimate sophistication.

— LEONARDO DA VINCI

When I first learned how to sell options for income, experienced traders said short-term out-of-the-money credit spreads on stocks would give me the highest probability of success. They strongly oppose the approach taught in this book: selling at-the-money put credit spreads. They adamantly claim that it has a low likelihood of success. Ironically, that is the exact approach that put the most money in my pocket. That's why I thought it fitting to end with a quick story so you understand why I was so willing to go against the status quo and ignore everyone who said I would fail.

I learned that sometimes probabilities can be wrong, but things still work out in your favor. For instance, I'm a minority who grew up poor in America. Our house had no running water or bathroom, and we used a five-gallon paint bucket as a toilet. Our only water source was a well with a hand pump attached to it. My dad died of cancer when I was eleven, and I was left to be raised by a mentally ill mom who abused me. I share all this not so you can feel sorry for me but to reinforce a point made earlier in the book: Probabilities are not a "guarantee."

The probabilities state that a kid who grew up like me is more likely to end up in jail than they are to be successful. Yet, despite my traumatic childhood, I became financially independent and left corporate America when I was thirty-four. I'm a statistical anomaly—an oddball who doesn't look like most in the investment community or have Ivy League credentials like most financial experts. My entire rise to prosperity has been unconventional. That's why it shouldn't be surprising that I'm introducing a new and unconventional way to sell credit spreads.

I'm one of the first, if not the first, to teach the approach of selling long-term at-the-money SPX put credit spreads. I fully expect this method to be criticized and its adoption slow. And that's okay. A critic's close-minded bigotry doesn't hurt me—it hurts them. It doesn't affect my profits; it affects theirs. A millionaire mentor told me to ignore what people say and listen to results because results don't lie. And the results of following the cash flow template have been phenomenal. I may not make a gazillion dollars a year, but I'm living my version of a dream lifestyle. And I'm not the only one—here's a note I recently received:

> *Thank you for making this possible for me. There's nothing like enjoying a vacation paid for in cash, not worrying about money or whether I can afford my bills afterward. I even made a little money while relaxing on the beach—none of which I could have done without you!*
>
> — BRITTANY W.

Brittany sent this note along with a photo. The first thing I noticed in the photo was the two cruise ships, clear blue ocean water, and sandy beach. Then I saw the caption under the picture: "I placed my monthly trade right in this spot." Here's the takeaway: If, like Brittany, you want to earn passive income while sitting on a beach, you should follow the simple four-step blueprint revealed in this book.

- Sell SPX put credit spreads in upward-trending markets.
- Limit your risk of loss with the 2/10 formula.
- Dollar-cost average with long-term at-the-money credit spreads.

- Lastly, automate the closing of profitable trades with "good-till-canceled" orders.

It's simple, effective, takes little time, and produces consistent income. I've yet to find anyone who dislikes the money earned from that process. However, if you are new to this, it will take about three to six months to get the hang of it and a few years of consistently showing up to master it. In other words, this book can't turn you into an investment pro; only real-world experience can do that.

The only way to experience the profit potential of credit spreads is to give the strategy a good, honest try. With the proof-of-concept exercise, the most you can lose is $5,000 and a few hours of your time. However, if it works for you, as it did for me, Brittany, and thousands of others ... you'll be able to turn ten minutes of free time into consistent cash flow each month. Imagine how good it will feel to live a ten-minute investor lifestyle. Just think about how much you will gain from having the ability to generate cash on demand without needing to get a second job. However, it can only happen if you make it happen. So if you're ready to make that lifestyle your reality, you know what to do ... Trust, but verify. Godspeed and I hope you enjoy the ride on the passive income train as much as I do.

One final word: If this book has helped you, I would appreciate it if you visited the store where you bought it and left a review. Reviews are the best way for independently published books to get noticed and reach more people like you who want to better their financial future. I read every review and welcome praise as well as constructive feedback. Your support makes a real difference and will help improve future books.

Finally, don't forget your book bonuses at www.trader travis.com/bookbonus.html.

REFERENCES

Baldwin, William. "Be Like Warren Buffett: Sell Put Options." *Forbes*, July 18, 2012. https://www.forbes.com/forbes/2012/0806/investing-crash-insurance-spdr-make-money-from-fear.html.

Chow, Alvin. "Warren Buffett Sold Naked Options." *Dr Wealth*, April 28, 2024. https://drwealth.com/warren-buffett-sold-naked-options.

Debt-Free Doctor. n.d. "25 Best Passive Income Quotes For Doctors." Accessed December 30, 2024. https://www.debtfreedr.com/passive-income-quotes-2/

InvestorPlace. "How Warren Buffett Made $7.5 Million by Failing." *Nasdaq*, June 15, 2017. https://www.nasdaq.com/articles/how-warren-buffett-made-75-million-failing-2017-06-15.

Jennewine, Taylor. "Here's the Average Stock Market Return in Every Month of the Year." *The Motley Fool*, February 6, 2024. https://www.fool.com/investing/2024/02/06/average-stock-market-return-in-every-month-of-year/.

Locke, Taylor. "3 Investing Lessons Warren Buffett Shared at the 2021 Berkshire Hathaway Meeting." *CNBC*, May 10, 2022. https://www.cnbc.com/2021/05/03/investing-lessons-from-warren-buffett-at-berkshire-hathaway-meeting.html.

Shareholder Letters. Accessed December 21, 2024. https://www.berkshirehathaway.com/letters/letters.html.

Wikipedia contributors. "Warren Buffett." *Wikipedia*, last modified December 2, 2024. https://en.wikipedia.org/wiki/Warren_Buffett.

Yahoo. "How Buffett Used 'Financial Weapons of Mass Destruction' to Make Billions of Dollars." Accessed December 21, 2024. https://finance.yahoo.com/news/how-buffett-used--financial-weapons-of-mass-destruction--to-make-billions-of-dollars-175922498.html.

Yahoo. "A Look Back at Warren Buffett's $37 Billion Stock Market Bet." Accessed December 21, 2024. https://finance.yahoo.com/news/look-back-warren-buffetts-37-172546595.html.

ABOUT THE AUTHOR

Travis Wilkerson, a.k.a. Trader Travis, is a US Army Veteran and 2019 United States Investing Champion (Options Division). For most of Travis's twenty-year trading career, he struggled with the question: How can a person who grew up poor, with no Wall Street connections, and only an average I.Q. at best, compete against the best and brightest of Wall Street? The answer is you don't!

In his book series, Travis will share the simple system he created for average, ordinary investors like himself. This system allowed him to win the US Investing Championship while only spending roughly ten minutes a day managing his options portfolio. He attributes his success to focusing on risk first and profits second. In addition, Travis has mentored thousands of trading students, teaching them the exact strategies he used to go from deep in debt to financially free in only five years.

You can connect with me on:

https://www.tradertravis.com

https://twitter.com/tradertravis

Subscribe to my newsletter:

https://www.tradertravis.com/bookbonus.html

Made in the USA
Monee, IL
16 May 2025

17614184R00115